Dr Richard Race.

What is Urban History?

What is History? series

John H. Arnold, *What is Medieval History?*

Peter Burke, *What is Cultural History?* 2nd edition

Peter Burke, *What is the History of Knowledge?*

John C. Burnham, *What is Medical History?*

Pamela Kyle Crossley, *What is Global History?*

Pero Gaglo Dagbovie, *What is African American History?*

Christine Harzig and Dirk Hoerder, with Donna Gabaccia, *What is Migration History?*

J. Donald Hughes, *What is Environmental History?* 2nd edition

Andrew Leach, *What is Architectural History?*

Stephen Morillo with Michael F. Pavkovic, *What is Military History?* 2nd edition

Sonya O. Rose, *What is Gender History?*

Brenda E. Stevenson, *What is Slavery?*

Richard Whatmore, *What is Intellectual History?*

What is Urban History?

Shane Ewen

polity

First published in 2016 by Polity Press

Polity Press
65 Bridge Street
Cambridge CB2 1UR, UK

Polity Press
350 Main Street
Malden, MA 02148, USA

ISBN-13: 978-0-7456-5268-9
ISBN-13: 978-0-7456-5269-6(pb)

A catalogue record for this book is available from the British Library.

Library of Congress Cataloging-in-Publication Data

Ewen, Shane.
  What is urban history? / Shane Ewen.
    pages cm. – (What is history)
  Includes bibliographical references and index.
    ISBN 978-0-7456-5268-9 (hardcover : alk. paper) – ISBN 0-7456-5268-9 (hardcover : alk. paper) – ISBN 978-0-7456-5269-6 (pbk. : alk. paper) – ISBN 0-7456-5269-7 (pbk. : alk. paper)   1. Cities and towns–Historiography.   2. Urbanization–Historiography.   I. Title.
  HT113.E94 2015
  307.7609–dc23
                              2015012742

Typeset in 10.5 on 12 pt Sabon
by Toppan Best-set Premedia Limited
Printed and bound in the UK by CPI Group (UK) Ltd. Croydon

Contents

Acknowledgements   vi

Introduction: Why Urban History?   1

1   The Development of Urban History   10

2   Cities, Spaces and Identities   33

3   Governing Cities   55

4   Cities and the Environment   75

5   Urban Culture and Modernity   92

6   Transnational Urban History   114

Notes   129
Suggestions for Further Reading   152
Index   158

Acknowledgements

I am indebted to a host of urban historians who have influenced me over the past fifteen years or more, during my intellectual journey through undergraduate and postgraduate study and into my current privileged position as a university lecturer. Nick Hayes was the first to introduce me to the study of municipal government and I am grateful to him for this and his ceaseless encouragement ever since. Richard Rodger was and remains an inspirational doctoral supervisor and 'urban guru', providing me with the freedom to develop my interests in comparative urban history. In addition, Roey Sweet and Dieter Schott were formative influences in the classroom for this postgraduate student who thought (incorrectly) that he knew everything! In fact, the organization and atmosphere of the Centre for Urban History at the University of Leicester inspires and cultivates a culture of inclusivity between staff and postgraduate students, as well as a critical and friendly exchange of ideas; it truly is the spiritual home for urban historians practising in the UK. Bob Morris proved to be an excellent mentor during my early career fellowship at the University of Edinburgh, encouraging me to widen my reading, much of which was done at the marvellous National Library of Scotland. It was during this period that I collaborated with Pierre-Yves Saunier on our global municipalities project, and Pierre-Yves' influence is discernible within this book and my most recent research. I have also received much great advice, inspiration and support over the years from, amongst others, Stefan Couperus, Krista Cowman, Barry Doyle, Geneviève Massard-Guilbaud, Simon Gunn, Rebecca Madgin, Helen Meller and Stana Nenadic. I am also grateful to colleagues (past and present) in the School of Cultural Studies and Humanities at Leeds Beckett University for their interest in and encouragement for my research, especially Franco Bianchini, Brian McCook, Stephen Mosley, Ruth Robbins and Heather Shore. I am hugely appreciative to Andrea Drugan at Polity Press for giving me the opportunity to immerse myself in such a rich scholarship in the first place; I am also particularly indebted and grateful to Elliott Karstadt for his encouragement and timely prompts to get it completed; without these I would still be writing! Thanks are also due to the anonymous readers for their encouraging comments on the original book proposal as well as an earlier draft manuscript. Finally, I am ever thankful to Sarah Bradbury for her untiring support during the past five years when, on occasion, it looked as if I would never complete the book.

I⟶ V. RAPID GROWTH OF URBANISATION,
      GLOBALLY

II⟶ { ECON DRIVERS OF URBANISATION
      { ÉCON HIST OF CITIES [⟵ GLAESER ⨎ CITIES]
                                    EFFICIENCY

II⟶ DIFF. PREMOD "CITIES" VS. LATE-MOD "MEGACITIES"

Introduction

Why Urban History?

This book does not purport to offer a history of towns and cities or the city-building process. As the recently published *Oxford Handbook of Cities in World History*, edited by Peter Clark, shows, this in itself is a gargantuan effort demanding the collaborative energy and expertise of fifty-six urban historians.[1] Instead, this book is intended as an introduction to the field of urban history, which, at its heart, is concerned with the study of urban life in the past as well as the history of urbanization (in its broadest understanding as a demographic, legal-institutional and cultural process). It is aimed at students who have already had training in history but have not previously studied urban history, as well as historians who have worked with towns and cities, but never from the perspective of an urban historian. What I mean by this is that urban history is concerned with examining the history of an urban place in the context of its wider economic, social, political, cultural and spatial system, which inevitably locates that place in a wider regional, national, international, and even transnational, network. The book is also aimed at students and other readers who have encountered towns and cities in other fields – such as geography, sociology, anthropology and town planning – and are interested in utilizing an historical approach to their subject.

This book stresses the mutual value of comparative and interdisciplinary approaches to understanding the spatial and experiential aspects of urban life. Such an integrated approach enables the systematic gathering of empirical evidence in order to identify what is common to the urban experience, as well as what sets one urban place aside from another. Interdisciplinarity is, as we shall see, essential to urban history because the field has grown up and evolved throughout the twentieth century by drawing upon multiple disciplinary influences from across the humanities as well as the social sciences. There is a tendency amongst some urban historians to interpret the field in largely social scientific terms, yet the truth is that urban history has drawn from a wide range of influences, approaches and traditions prevalent across the arts and humanities as well as the 'soft' sciences, including art, literature, photography, archaeology, cultural and film studies, which have injected the field with a critical mass and rich texture of styles and sources. A cursory read of recent studies by scholars working with issues of urban culture and materiality reveals the eclectic source base from which practitioners are working, and the reader's attention is drawn to the 'Suggestions for Further Reading' chapter at the end of this book for examples of these.

Comparative approaches are themselves central to explaining historical continuities as well as change, and have been widely deployed within a range of historical fields that have helped to shape urban history, including economic and social history, historical sociology and the French Annales School. Comparative method helps the historian to discover the similarities as well as the uniqueness of different societies through time and across space. The historical sociologist Charles Tilly contends that comparison, over long periods of time as well as across space, empowers the urban historian to answer the central historical questions in academic scholarship, and to explore the interaction between large global processes as well as the everyday routines and rhythms of urban life. For urban historians, comparison illustrates how all towns and cities share common requirements throughout history: they all need resources (food, water, raw materials and people) to sustain their growth. They also need a viable economic function, access to commercial networks that connect them with a wider region, and organizational stability and security provided by supportive administrative, fiscal and legal frameworks. As Penelope Corfield persuasively argues, these features indicate that towns and cities enjoy 'deep continuities' in their location, functionality, topography and social/cultural traditions even if they also expand, contract and redevelop over time. Comparison – in its diachronic as well as its synchronic sense – reveals how 'becoming globally urban is one of our great collective achievements through time'.[2]

It is my contention that urban history is of increasing significance in today's urban world. While there is a growing importance for conducting international comparisons of towns and cities, invariably of a typological kind, the real everyday strengths of the comparative approach – due to the logistical and historical/cultural traditions of urban history – remains most fruitful in a national framework. However, the incentive of international and transnational comparison is significant, especially between the fast-growing megacities and mega-regions in the developing world – from Latin America and the Indian subcontinent to China and the Middle East – and well-established and networked cities in the developed world. This sort of cross-continental research offers benefits for the researcher to situate his or her research into a wider socio-political exchange that could materially benefit the residents of these megacities, but also those in the developed world. Urban history offers valuable lessons if one looks for them, and urban historians invariably do this on a daily basis – in how to govern cities in order to fairly tackle the vast inequalities of urban capitalism; how to identify and minimize the environmental hazards of rapid urbanization if left to the vagaries of the marketplace; and of the importance of culture, nature and planning to make cities attractive places to live and work in or travel to.

The centrality of urbanization to the world today, and its rooting in history, has been summarized in a series of reports from the United Nations Human Settlements Programme (UN-Habitat). Whereas only a century ago, two out of every ten people in the world were living in urban areas – and in the least developed regions the proportion of urban dwellers was as low as 5 per cent – in 2011 the majority of the world's population was living in urban areas for the first time in human history (the proportion stands at 54 per cent in 2014).

Much of this recent growth, since the 1950s, has occurred in developing countries. In 2013, of every ten urban residents in the world more than seven could be found in developing countries. In the past decade alone, the urban population in the developing world grew by an average of 1.2 million people *every week* (this amounts to slightly less than a full year's growth across urban Europe). Asia led the way, adding 0.88 million new urban dwellers *every week*, followed by Africa, with an additional 0.23 million *every week*, and Latin America and the Caribbean with 0.15 million *every week*. Latin America is the second most urbanized region in the world today, with 80 per cent of its population living in urban areas; North America remains the most urbanized region (82 per cent), while Europe lies in third place (73 per cent). While Africa and Asia remain predominantly rural continents, with 40 and 48 per cent of their respective populations living in urban areas, they are urbanizing at a faster rate than all other regions and are projected to have urban populations of 56 and 64 per cent respectively by 2050.[3]

These rates of growth have generated a growing 'urban divide' between rich and poor. This is discernible through the unequal distribution of wealth and the persistence of socio-spatial segregation, which, comparison shows us, is evident in developed and developing cities alike and has been a constant feature of the urbanization process throughout history. It has also generated huge inequalities in social and environmental justice – for women, the disabled and ethnic, religious and sexual minorities, and so on. Cities are divided between 'haves' and 'have-nots' through competition over land, labour and capital, which produces social instability as well as considerable costs for the urban poor and society at large. But this is not a new challenge, as UN-Habitat recognizes; cities have always been subject to extreme levels of inequality and social deprivation: 'Cities do not become divisive overnight;...exclusion and marginalization build and reproduce over time.' Nor have cities responded to these challenges through history in the same way: this is because improvements (in infrastructure, governance, social justice and quality of life) are dependent on public demand, civil rights, existing knowledge and a city's access to institutional and financial resources, all of which vary over time. Urban history thus provides an ideal outlet for policymakers to learn from the past because it is a field that is grounded in comparison and interdisciplinarity and has always reflected contemporary concerns about urban society. Indeed, urban historians are naturally 'present-minded', pursuing topics that are relevant to the world that we live in and using history as a route into examining contemporary urban problems.[4]

History also reveals changes in the ranking of cities according to their size, significance and reach, as documented in Tertius Chandler and Gerald Fox's historical census of urban growth. In the early eighteenth century, Constantinople and Beijing were the two largest cities in the world, with populations of roughly 700,000; a century later, Beijing and London had both topped 1 million. By the turn of the twentieth century, the era of the Western metropolis had arrived: London was the largest city with 6.48 million residents, followed by New York (4.24 million), Paris (3.33 million), Berlin (2.42 million) and Chicago (1.72 million). Sixteen cities in total had populations of more than 1 million at this time, and the list was dominated by European and American cities. By 1950, although Western cities (New York, London, Paris) still dominated the top end of the table, Tokyo (or the Tokyo-Yokohama agglomeration) was the third largest city region in the world (c.7 million), while a number of developing cities were creeping up the league table (including Shanghai, Buenos Aires, Calcutta, Bombay, Mexico City, Rio de Janeiro and São Paulo). In 2011 there were nearly 500 cities and urban agglomerations (that is, a central city and neighbouring communities linked to it by continuous built-up areas) with populations exceeding 1 million, and twenty-six megacities exceeding 10 million. Tokyo is the largest city with an agglomeration of 38 million inhabitants, followed by Delhi (25 million), Shanghai (23 million), and Mexico City, Mumbai and São Paulo (each with around 21 million inhabitants). By 2030, the United Nations estimates, there will be forty-one megacities in the world, the vast majority of which will be found in developing countries. This shows that cities, and the networks that they constitute, are always changing, which establishes the value of comparison over time in order to understand what motivates people to relocate to urban areas at particular times in their life cycles in order to ride what Peter Clark has described as the 'rollercoaster' of urbanization.[5]

Cities have even started to merge together to create new spatial configurations, linked by their functional and spatial connections, which are expected to drive this rollercoaster over the next fifty years. These include mega-regions of large cities (Bangalore, Mexico City and Cairo, for example) which amalgamate other cities and towns within their economic orbit; urban corridors that link two or more large cities, sometimes across national borders – examples include Mumbai–Delhi, São Paulo–Rio de Janeiro and Ibadan–Lagos–Accra – and state-sponsored city-regions like Guangdong's Pearl River Delta mega-region, which includes nine large cities with an aggregate surface area of $40,000\,km^2$, or twenty-six times that of Greater London. Such staggering rates of growth obviously attract considerable interest in the past histories of the urban world, particularly in tracing the ways that cities and urban cultures have adapted to major social, economic, political, cultural and environmental change. There is a connection here between regions with fast-urbanizing populations and emerging scholarly interest in urban history. Whereas the origins and early growth of urban history as a scholarly discipline are to be found in Western and Northern Europe, as well as North America, the field continues to grow and develop in emerging regions, notably India, China and Latin America, albeit with their own unique traditions of scholarly practice.[6]

The book is organized thematically according to the main historiographical debates that have shaped the field over the past generation. Chapter 1 provides a chronological framework for the development of urban history since the turn of the twentieth century, and introduces key historiographical influences in the field. Chapter 2 examines the relationship between space and social identity through the lens of residential segregation, one of the richest subjects within the field. Chapter 3 traces changing approaches to how urban societies are governed, establishing the theoretical influences over the field at large, especially since the 1980s. The theme of environmental history is discussed in Chapter 4, particularly focusing on the value of an urban approach to interrogate the relationship between nature, materiality and the built environment. Chapter 5 then considers the impact of the cultural turn on urban cultures, specifically through an examination of the rich literature on urban modernity. Chapter 6 discusses the nascent influence of transnational approaches on urban history, which point towards a fruitful future in tracing networked urban histories that traverse the world and are not constrained by nation-state boundaries. Finally, a brief essay provides a guide for further reading and should be read in conjunction with the endnotes to individual chapters.

Unfortunately, it has not proven possible, in the limited space available, to provide a comprehensive treatment of all the themes that entertain urban historians. There are a couple of notable omissions. First, the role played by the urban economy in driving urban change is not treated separately in its own chapter, although, as this introduction argues, economic factors are a driving force throughout the history of urbanization. Having said this, the external forces that shaped the emergence of a global urban-industrial economy – or the more recent process of de-industrialization in the Western world – are not given as much treatment as some readers might like, though the book does take a 'political economy' approach to the city and municipal authorities. This decision is itself a reflection of the recent shift in focus from economic to cultural history, which is discernible in the tables of contents for the leading scholarly journals in the field and the conference programmes of the scholarly institutions. However, this should not be misinterpreted as a positive shift, not least because of the continued importance of cities to the global economy in the light of the economic crisis of recent years. Thus, in its 2010–11 report on the world's cities, UN-Habitat rightly recognizes cities as the key drivers of economic recovery, and their pivotal role in redressing the major inequalities that shape modern cities. Recent studies of the urban economy by David Reeder and Richard Rodger and Ho-Fung Hung and Shaohua Zhan, as well as Paul Bairoch's statistically rich *longue durée* history, provide excellent overviews of urban economic and demographic change that complement this book because they too examine urban economic processes through a comparative and interdisciplinary framework.[7]

Second, the book is overwhelmingly concerned with the modern city and the majority of examples discussed cover the past three hundred years or thereabouts. There are peda-gogical and organizational reasons for this decision. It would be shallow to attempt to provide comprehensive coverage of the ancient, medieval or early modern city when there are far more competent historians able to do this. As Rosemary Sweet and Richard Rodger discuss, the medieval or early modern town was 'a very different phenomenon' to its modern counterpart. For instance, there are major defini-tional disagreements about what actually constitutes urban status and how this changes over time and from country to country. In the pre-modern age, few towns exceeded 10,000 people, and are alien in contrast to those megacities that have mushroomed since the 1950s. It is a challenge in itself to determine what constitutes an urban area in the modern age, especially when variations in rates of urbanization in the nineteenth and early twentieth centuries were based on dif-ferent size thresholds, ranging from 2,000 in France to 20,000 in Italy.

Furthermore, most towns in the pre-modern period (outside the capital cities) were essentially part of an agrarian economy and should be treated as such, whereas many modern towns and cities can be studied as part of an urban-industrial economy, albeit one that owes its growth to mod-ernization in agriculture, as well as high rates of rural-to-urban migration. Finally, the value systems of medieval and early modern towns have often clashed with those of the modern period. Whereas issues of kinship, family and religion have been central to the earlier period, the modern period has been dominated by questions of class until recent years. While there has been recent convergence between the early modern and modern period through the scrutiny of alternative forms of social identity (noticeably gender and sexuality), it has been decided to focus on the modern period for reasons of academic coherence as well as convenience.[8]

To those readers who will now be considering returning the book to their library or to the bookshop for a refund, I ask for forgiveness and understanding. This book does not intend to provide an exhaustive account of urbanization throughout history – nor, come to that, of the field in its vast temporal, geographical, thematic and methodological reach – for that would demand resources, time, expertise and an additional 700 pages or more that are not at my disposal. Rather more modestly perhaps, but nonetheless of tangible value, I hope, I offer my interpretation of the vast, rich and evolving historiography of the urban world. Finally, I trust that this book will serve as a useful starting point for those beginning their intellectual (and actual) wanderings through the concrete jungle.

The Development of Urban History

...in this country, it's an almost inevitable choice, if one is a
historian interested in social change, in local politics, or in the
built form of the environment in one way or another, it is natural
to be drawn into, or become committed to the study of urban
life and its institution.[1]

So said H. J. Dyos in a conversation with Bruce Stave, published in 1979. These comments owed little to Britain's status
as one of the most urbanized nations in modern times because
urban history had parlous beginnings there compared to
Germany, the Low Countries and the United States, where
scholarship could be traced back to the early twentieth
century. Rather, they were a reflection of Dyos's pragmatic
approach to injecting an eclectic field with a set of shared
principles. By stressing the elasticity between multiple fields
and approaches in twentieth-century historiography, Dyos
helped establish urban history at the intersection of the arts
and humanities and the social sciences by insisting that the
experiential nature of urban life, its lived reality as well as
its representation, was as important as the building process.[2]

For Dyos and others like him, towns and cities are historical entities that act on the world around them in much the
same way as an electrical transformer stimulates human
interactions and exchanges. As 'agents of modernization',
towns and cities play a fundamental role in linking rural
communities and adjacent towns into a coherent social and

economic system, which is increasingly international in its connections. As Fernand Braudel, the Annales historian, put it in his study of capitalism in early modern Southern Europe, 'Toute ville est, se veut un monde à part' ('Every town is and wishes to be a separate world'). The implication here is that 'the town should be more than the sum of the parts from which it is constituted': it acts as both an independent variable in its own right and part of a wider system of urbanization.[3]

We can also detect within Dyos's comments some of the tensions and contradictions over what constitutes urban history as a distinct field and, in particular, what sets it apart from a more encompassing field like social history. Some critics have complained that urban historians fail to distinguish their work from social or economic history; they stress that cities are little more than stages upon which social or economic actors perform. In 1971, for example, Eric Hobsbawm likened urban history to 'a historical variety store' within which 'everything about cities' was up for inclusion; while Sidney Pollard, two years later, described the field as a synonym for social history: 'apart from some specific aspects of rural life like agriculture, modern British social history *is* urban history'.[4]

The reality is that urban history and social history are siblings, having grown up together under the parentage of economic history. They are, therefore, subject to the sort of petty squabbles that naturally exist between siblings, but which are outweighed by familial bonds. Both fields seek to explain human experience predominantly through a focus on 'history from below'; that is, of examining the role that ordinary people played as agents in the making of their own history, constrained by economic forces, the agents of social reproduction and the regulating role of the state. Yet urban history differs in one fundamental way to its sibling here: for the urban historian approaches the city in its totality, in producing 'whole' histories of the ways that a city has, in the words of Dolores Hayden, been 'planned, designed, built, inhabited, appropriated, celebrated, despoiled and discarded'.[5] The urban historian considers the multiple variables that together constitute the city as both a historicized subject and an object for historical study. The city is thus accorded an agency in its own construction and synthesis; its spaces, both imagined and real, shape, structure and represent the human relationships that take place within its borders.

This chapter will examine some of these themes. The origins and growth of urban history will be charted and the field's interdisciplinarity outlined. Urban history has, since the 1950s and 1960s at least, enjoyed an elastic boundary, allowing its protagonists to draw upon new theoretical or methodological innovations elsewhere, while also actively inviting visitors to contribute to their discussions. But this is not a boundaryless interdisciplinarity; urban history has enjoyed various epistemological, organizational and professional features that have given it form and identity as a field of historical scholarship. It has its own scholarly network of conferences, periodicals, book series and electronic discussion lists. Indeed, its interdisciplinary ethos is, as we shall see, a fundamental feature of its disciplinarity. Finally, the chapter will examine some of the more recent transitions within the field, including the rise of cultural history since the 1990s and, more recently still, the 'urban turn' in India, China and the developing world, which have served to further stretch the field's elasticity.

Urban History at the Turn of the Twentieth Century

Interest in the history of towns and cities is, it is fair to say, as old as the process of urbanization itself. Much of the eighteenth- and nineteenth-century interest in the development of towns and cities came from fields that were not traditionally considered part of mainstream history's remit, including antiquarianism, civic biography and local history. However, the expansion of historical interest intensified in the decades around the turn of the twentieth century; simultaneously, phenomenal rates of urbanization were brought on by industrialization, immigration and state reforms within the Western European and North American nations, as well as Japan and Russia. Many of the earliest writings thereby reflected a great concern for cities and their 'problems', and were strongly influenced by a drive to observe, categorize and reform the contemporary urban condition. For example, while there is a long tradition, dating from the mid-nineteenth century, of German historical interest in medieval towns, the explosion of scholarly interest in urban history was a more recent phenomenon following national unification in the 1870s.[6] The same can be said about historical interest in towns in the Low Countries, where the work of Henri Pirenne in the early twentieth century was significant in revealing the long-term histories of towns as mercantile communities with their own institutions from as early as the thirteenth century.[7]

It is no coincidence that historical interest in the urban condition mirrored a simultaneous interest in town planning, municipalization and philanthropy in Western European countries. As Daniel Roche has written in relation to France, historical interest combined nostalgia for a past which appeared richer than the present with 'a dream of a city of the future, capable of reconciling community and social control, nature and culture'.[8] Contemporaneous town-planning interests, like the garden city movement in Britain, shared a similar nostalgia for a traditional, rural way of life mixed with the social and economic realities of the modern urban condition. This combination of traditional and modern styles inevitably converged on the city as the site for new physical, spatial and experiential relationships, and which, as discussed in chapter 5, was the centre of modernity in the early twentieth century.

Much of this early historical interest in cities was, therefore, stimulated by contemporary anxieties about urban problems posed by overcrowding, poverty and unsanitary environments, as well as the drive to initiate a more systematic and planned society; this helps to explain why urban historians continue to be animated by urban problems in cities today. This diverse literature – a mixture of polemical and imperialist rhetoric about class, degeneration and race, and serious scientific and philanthropic studies of poverty and ill health – has been charted by Andrew Lees. The rise of large industrial cities in Britain, Germany, France and the United States attracted a considerable fervour of interest from contemporary writers whose first-hand observations reveal the multiple ways that urbanization was intellectually and culturally perceived. For example, German anti-urban writers like Georg Hansen expressed their fears about the physiological and demographic impact of urbanization as a threat to their new nation-state's racial purity, whereas populist British writers like Robert Blatchford cited urbanization as the root cause of moral and physical degeneration amongst the working classes.

It was not all doom and gloom, however. Intellectual interest was also stimulated by an innate belief in the economic, social and cultural benefits to be accrued from urban life, held by many people. These included the French economist and geographer Émile Levasseur and his student Paul Meuriot, both of whom were working in the 1890s. Levasseur believed that modern cities like Paris helped the nation to maintain a social equilibrium by absorbing the rapidly growing population and contributing to economic growth. Meuriot, too, argued that the growth of cities provided alternative opportunities for migrants from the countryside other than emigration. Meuriot gathered statistics on the urban development of European countries in order to study the growth of 'urban agglomerations' as a continental-wide phenomenon during the nineteenth century, identifying this transformation in the structure of society as unparalleled in earlier times because of the technological and economic changes wrought by coal and steam.[9]

We can, therefore, locate the origins of scholarly urban history at the intersection of the humanities and social sciences. This interest in the growth of cities represented as much a mental transformation in human culture as a response to a demographic and economic phenomenon that could be mapped statistically. Contemporary authors, including Georg Simmel, Walter Benjamin, Max Weber and Louis Wirth, conceived of the city in socio-psychological and structural/functional terms. Simmel, for one, identified 'metropolitan man' as a creature of urban modernity, in which the individual, to avoid being completely overwhelmed by the pressures of modern life, embraced the characteristics of punctuality, calculation and precision, alongside an exacting obsession with time and the discipline of the clock. Weber, meanwhile, saw the transactional and depersonalized nature of modern economic and social relationships as key to explaining the growing anonymity of urban populations.[10]

There is also an in-built tendency, amongst modern urban historians at least, to utilize social-scientific models in order to provide more generalized accounts of the urbanization process. An early pioneer was the economist Adna Ferrin Weber, who took a statistical approach to categorize the growth of modern cities country by country. This included detailed breakdowns of changes in city populations, as well as their distribution and ranking within the urban system. Moreover, he documented the advantages of modern urban life over the countryside with reference to Charles Darwin's work, explaining that the city offered certain economic, educational and cultural opportunities that the village could never provide. In so doing, cities were 'the instruments of natural selection', performing a service in 'weeding out the incapable and inefficient, while advancing the more capable members of society'.[11]

Similarly, Max Weber was interested in the Western city as a model of historical development from medieval times, which reflected his wider concern about the function and organization of urban-industrial society at the turn of the twentieth century. In *The City*, posthumously published, Weber mapped the modern city from ancient times as a system of social actions, relationships and institutions that constituted an urban community with common features and functions. These included fortification, a market, a court of its own and a partially autonomous legal system, as well as an associative and administrative character within which the burgher class of property owners and rate-payers participated. What distinguished the European city from its counterparts in the Middle East and Asia, Weber argued, were its comparatively well-developed levels of urban political autonomy, alongside a distinctive civic and communal identity. This has gone on to shape subsequent scholarship of Asian cities, especially in the Islamic world.[12]

In addition to these intellectual influences over urban research during the twentieth century, historians cite large city events such as the 1910 and 1912 town-planning exhibitions, in Berlin and Düsseldorf respectively, as further evidence of this emerging social-scientific field of interest. These events, along with others like the International Exposition held at Ghent in 1913, stimulated the international exchange and circulation of models of urban reform and planning. In studying the development of towns over time, as well as the organization and management of communal or municipal life, such events inevitably attracted the intrinsic interest of the urban historian: Henri Pirenne even sat on the Ghent Exposition's organizing committee, further illustrating urban historians' thirst for linking the history of urban communities with contemporary social and political issues.[13]

The growing international connections between cities and the study of urbanization inevitably shaped the growth of the field in developed and developing countries alike. This is evident in the experience of small countries like the Scandinavian nations, where rapid urbanization and industrialization in the early twentieth century generated a parallel interest in urban history. In Sweden, for instance, an Institute of Urban History was founded as early as 1919 as a section of the Confederation of Swedish Towns, from which there emerged a strong interest in town growth and administration from historians such as Nils Herlitz and Nils Ahnlund. Meanwhile, a long tradition of scholarly interest in urban history in Norway and Finland has been explained by their late national independence, in 1905 and 1917 respectively, as well as their subsequent urbanization during the first half of the twentieth century.[14]

Urban History in North America: The Growth of an Interdisciplinary Phenomenon

This mutual interest in the city as a contemporary and historical issue is exemplified in the rise of urban history in North America between the 1920s and 1960s. For example, the work of the 'Chicago School' at the University of Chicago, notably Robert Park, Ernest Burgess and Louis Wirth, pioneered the idea of using the city as a laboratory to explore the changing patterns and experiences of human society and culture. They established the significance of cities as objects of study and offered theoretical models against which empirical data could be tested. They also used the city as a vehicle for studying social structure and its practices; urban life was best understood as embedded in its wider geographic and material environment. As Thomas Gieryn has shown, their researchers conducted field observations in the city, transforming the city of Chicago into a laboratory where knowledge about social life could be generated and mapped: 'Chicago School urban studies were in Chicago, of Chicago, and about Chicago.' In this respect, then, the city became a 'truth spot' in which 'being there' became 'an essential part of claiming authority for an observation or discovery', by subjecting the city to scientific measurement, experiment and categorization.[15]

The Chicago School's work subsequently proved decisive in establishing the connection between history and the social sciences in North America, particularly in examining the different ways that a city's social structure and its use of space changed over time. For example, Arthur Schlesinger, Sr, experimented with the idea of the city as a laboratory for social research while at graduate school in Columbus, Ohio, where he first encountered sociological and geographical approaches to studying cities. His subsequent publications, notably *The Rise of the City, 1878–1989*, drew upon these new methodologies to provide the first detailed study of urban-industrial changes in late nineteenth-century America. They were subsequently followed by studies from, amongst others, Richard Wade, Bayrd Still and Blake McKelvey, while later generations of urban historians, Eric Lampard and Sam Bass Warner, Jr, included, cite Schlesinger as a major influence during the isolated years of the fledgling field's history.[16]

The evolving social science disciplines of the mid-twentieth century provided fertile breeding ground for urban historians. Widespread contemporary interest in the pathological aspects of urban life and the effects of post-war planning on everyday life blurred the distinction between popular and scholarly studies, and folded the multiple disciplinary approaches into a more general and accessible critique of urban policymaking. A new generation of activists and writers, frustrated by the limited accomplishments of the post-war world, appeared with a passion for cities as vibrant engines of social and cultural life, a commitment to the emerging movements for preservation and conservation, and a frustration at the destructive nature of downtown redevelopment and suburban sprawl. They were united by their frustration and anger at what they saw as the increasingly disinterested activities of the 'urbanist establishment', or what Christopher Klemek has called the 'urban renewal order', of expert planners, architects and designers, who they felt were out of step with public opinion.[17] Jane Jacobs's *The Death and Life of Great American Cities*, Jean Gottmann's *Megalopolis*, and Lewis Mumford's *The City in History* were all published in 1961, and called for a fundamental rethinking of city planning, establishing a precedent for urban historians by using examples from the past as lessons for the dangers of reconstruction without citizen participation. Jacobs critiqued post-war urban policy, finding modernist planners responsible for the destruction of urban communities through the construction of isolated urban neighbourhoods. In particular, she cited the destruction of the street and the sidewalk – which she described as 'the nervous system' of the city – in favour of high-rise apartment blocks and the unfettered embrace of the automobile as heralding the death of downtown.[18]

Gottmann, meanwhile, identified the various planning and administrative problems posed by the emerging north-eastern metropolitan seaboard of the United States, which extended from Boston, Massachusetts, through New York, Philadelphia, Baltimore, and ended in Washington, DC, and Northern Virginia. UN-Habitat's recent studies of mega-regions obviously owe a great debt to this in the framing of new spatial configurations and their subsequent conceptualization.[19] Moreover, the historian and sociologist Lewis Mumford, who had warned about the dangers of over-development in the late 1930s, prophetically predicted the coming of necropolis in an age where urban culture was being increasingly usurped by technological innovation. For Mumford, the sprawling megalopolis was at risk of the same fate that befell the Roman city if its civic leaders and planners failed to strike a balance between the organic nature of urban growth and the physical design of modern planning.[20] The modern city was becoming, in the words of another contemporary writer, a place of extreme social inequality, in which the wealthy, driven by a 'glorified provincialism', fled from the city for the monotony of suburbia ('the land of blue jeans and shopping centers [*sic*]'), where they lived side by side with the same planners who were redeveloping the old downtown areas with super-blocks and islands of social deprivation cut off from each other by freeways and underpasses. Similar, albeit more nuanced, critiques were being advanced in Western Europe, with periodicals like the *Architectural Review* (UK) and *Bauwelt* (West Berlin) championing the idea of 'multiple use' (mixing functions in a building or area) rather than the sort of functional segregation and zoning practised by modern urbanists.[21]

These polemical studies inevitably stimulated historical interest in seeking to explain the 1960s as a decade of urban crisis. There was something intrinsically modern about this phenomenon, especially when Oscar Handlin confidently mapped out a research programme for the modern city as 'a field of historical study'. This was manifestly an interdisciplinary field since Handlin drew upon the work of the Webers, Mumford, the geographer Gideon Sjoberg and the political scientist William Robson to make the case that the modern industrial city was radically different from its earlier counterpart and, as such, could only be studied in relation to the wider world within which it was situated, rather than as 'a world unto itself': 'Large enough to have a character of its own, the modern city is yet inextricably linked to, dependent upon, the society outside it; and growth in size has increased rather than diminished the force of that dependence.'[22] This was subsequently reinforced at an international conference on 'The Study of Urbanization' held at the University of Chicago in 1965 and sponsored by the American Social Science Research Council. It included talks from geographers and historians, who, having formed a joint Committee of Urbanization, recommended future scholars to 'work toward the advancement of multi-disciplinary research in the process of urbanization'.[23]

Having established the city as a legitimate subject for historical inquiry, this new generation of scholars combined the best elements of empirical history with the rigorous methodologies provided through theoretical testing, quantification and comparison. Their work stood at the vanguard of postwar historical research, in pushing the boundaries of accepted historical practice, and in utilizing new technologies like card indexing and computing. As a result, a 'new urban history' had emerged by the late 1960s, with a more specialized focus on quantifying the urban experience from the 'bottom-up', with notable studies appearing by, amongst others, Stephan Thernstrom, Eric Monkkonen and Kathleen Conzen. The emphasis of this new literature was on using published censuses to track the social mobility of classes and ethnic groups within individual cities. Their preference for smaller cities – Thernstrom's study focuses on Newburyport, Massachusetts, for instance – further reflected an emerging interest in understudied places.[24]

Others, however, were less convinced that anything radically new had emerged. For example, in an interview with Bruce Stave, published in the first issue of the *Journal of Urban History*, which was launched in 1974, Warner professed to stumbling into 'what later became a field', and denied being able to research or teach urban history without borrowing from other fields. He further warned against the sort of urban history that involved studying social groups who happened to reside in cities. Urban historians, he argued, should conceive of the city in totality, and explore the political, economic, social and spatial systems of cities, both individually and comparatively; the city was an actor in its own making and remaking.[25] Such a view chimed with that of H. J. Dyos and the Leicester school of urban history in Britain, to which we now turn.

The 'Dyos Phenomenon' in Britain

To many British urban historians, Dyos was the doyen of urban history. According to David Reeder, his 'single-minded commitment' to the city made Dyos 'a leading figure in the burgeoning field of urban history during the 1960s'.[26] He has been described as, simultaneously, the parent *and* midwife of an entire field (he is more often referred to as the 'father' of urban history).[27] He was the first professor of urban history in England (at the University of Leicester, 1971), was the founder and editor of the *Urban History Newsletter* (1962) and *Urban History Yearbook* (1974, which later became

Urban History), edited a series of books on urban history, and organized the annual conferences of the Urban History Group from 1963 until his early death in 1978. His archive of personal and professional papers, catalogued by researchers at the university's Centre for Urban History, has been made available for study and has even attracted doctoral studies of the origins and development of urban history in Britain.[28]

Dyos was also the author of one of the most influential urban history monographs, *Victorian Suburb: A Study of the Growth of Camberwell*, also published in 1961, which defined the field of study for later generations of scholars and remains required reading on course reading lists. In the book, he mapped out the main contours of the field, establishing the importance of studying the grand processes of population growth and urbanization, as well as the individual experience of living in an urban place. These grand processes included industrialization, suburbanization and municipalization; the shape of the modern city was, after all, based upon capitalist enterprise and the spatial segregation produced by the speculative development and regulation of slums and suburbs.

Yet these processes were themselves the products of human action. As Dyos notes, 'The makers of the Victorian suburb were a mixed and very numerous company, in which must be numbered not only those who were recognizably in the suburb-building business, but many others whose contribution to the structure of the suburb appeared remote or insignificant.'[29] This meant that it was equally important to study the landowners, speculative builders, financiers, service providers and urban residents themselves, in order to understand the human relationships within these containing forces. This subsequently revealed how the character of a place became distinctive, while also retaining connections to the wider social and cultural trends of the time. As Dyos himself put it in his 'Agenda to Urban Historians', which was part of the published proceedings of an international round-table conference at the University of Leicester in September 1966:

> The study of urban history must mean not merely the study of individual communities, fixed more or less in time and space – what might be called the urban aspect of local history; but the investigation

of altogether broader historical processes and trends that completely transcend the life cycle and range of experiences of particular communities.[30]

To put it more simply, urban historians are interested in the interaction of people with the urban fabric that they live and work in. An urban approach allows the historian to explain a particular city's present condition in the context of those historical forces that shaped it.

By the time of his inaugural lecture in 1973, Dyos was dogmatically celebrating urban history's interdisciplinarity and its multi-centredness: 'Urban history, it must by now be clear, is a field of knowledge, not a single discipline in the accepted sense but a field in which many disciplines converge, or at any rate are drawn upon.'[31] This meant, in practice, that urban history (as a formal academic church) comprised a relatively small congregation of devout parishioners, but that its sphere of influence drew widely from across different faiths. What mattered was the interest in the totality of the city and its connections with the wider context rather than the specific methodological approach being taken. Dyos later commented that, although urban history had lost its raggedness during the 1970s, thanks to the emergence of a more coherent scholarly identity through its conferences, periodicals and book series, '[i]t would be a gross conceit to pretend that it did somehow have a distinctive discipline'. Instead, he asserted, it should be seen as 'a kind of strategy' preoccupied with current issues explored historically.[32] For Dyos, however, 'the city' explored through time was the sole criterion for an urban approach towards history. These could be explored comparatively, as individual city biographies, or as part of the broader 'city family', but they should be interactive and analytical.

Ways of Doing Urban History

This commitment to grand process and place has continued to shape urban history. In *The Pursuit of Urban History*, edited by Anthony Sutcliffe and Derek Fraser to take stock of the field in the years following Dyos's death, Sydney Checkland persuasively describes 'the urban historian proper'

as one who embraces the 'containing context' of social, economic, spatial and political systems with the biographical or
comparative city case study. He cites numerous examples of
historians who all utilize the city case study, both as a biographical study of what I call the place-in-context, but also
as a comparison between places, in order to reveal 'a range
of cities formed and functioning under shared circumstances'.
This subsequently allows for a comparison of urban structure, function and performance, as well as common urban
problems and the paths adopted in tackling them.[33]

Other historians, David Reeder and Richard Rodger
included, established the value of multi-authored urban biographies, which increasingly locate their cities as members of
a historical family. Such studies offer serious biographies
of individual cities as social entities and in different phases
of their history, alert to both the particularities of place and
the wider operation of power in the urban system.[34] In similar
vein, collaborative approaches to urban history, despite their
logistical and technical difficulties, also point towards a
further expansion in cross-national urban biography and
comparison with new publications appearing on comparative
and transnational approaches that situate the city in its widest
context, but without losing focus on the independent urban
variable.[35]

Urban biographies and comparative urban histories tend
to be situated within a typological framework (or the family
idiom as described by Checkland) based on urban scale
(capital cities, second cities, megacities and the like), function
(ports, industry, mining, spas and tourist centres, etc.), categories (Mediterranean cities, manufacturing cities, Canadian prairie cities and British new towns, for example), and
thematic studies based around demography, transport, government regulation, income and occupational patterns. This
has enabled urban historians to move away from the purely
local study to situate those peculiarities in a wider networked
history of flows, connections and patterns of urbanization
and urban growth. The port cities' literature has been particularly good at examining the linkages between different
seaports as nodes in a wider international and cosmopolitan
network that transcends national cultures to produce their
own cultural, political, social and economic practices. As

Carola Hein describes it, the urban environment and human relationships of the port city is the product of 'specific local constellations of actors, of their relation to the foreland and the hinterland, as well as of global transformation'. They are built on trade and exchange networks between specific cities around the world and, with the comparison between port cities that this necessitates, it is possible to trace the combination of global transformation and local initiative that has shaped the multiple layers of the built and social environment.[36]

Scholarly periodicals like *Urban History*, the *Journal of Urban History*, and *Urban History Review/Revue d'histoire urbaine* (the Canadian journal of urban history, founded in 1972) reflect this emphasis on examining the place-in-context. They have continually published articles on a variety of related topics, combining an interest in macro social and economic systems with micro studies of everyday aspects of the urban experience. They are pledged to publishing articles that take interdisciplinary and comparative approaches towards the study of urban history; papers include comparisons of town or city development over time; comparisons of towns or cities within a country, or even, as is increasingly the case, across national borders.[37] Intercultural comparisons have also emerged in recent decades, and a perusal of the tables of contents reveals a growing propensity to publish research articles on the cultural histories of towns and cities with a particular focus on the interdependence of gender, sexuality, ethnicity and class. This is symptomatic of a wider shift towards cultural analysis in history, which has had a marked influence on urban history.

The 'Cultural Turn' in Urban History

Dyos himself, along with Michael Wolff, made the first significant contribution to the cultural history of cities, with a two-volume collection of essays, *The Victorian City: Images and Realities*, published in 1973 with a rich tapestry of visual sources, including maps, photographs and artwork, to accompany the chapters. Drawing together scholars from across the humanities and social sciences, initially in Bloomington, Indiana, for a Victorian Studies Symposium in 1967, it was one of the first histories to cover people's perceptions of urban life alongside the social and economic realities of migration, poverty, property speculation and planning. In that respect, it reflected Dyos's conviction that the urban historian should historicize the city in its cultural, as well as its social and economic, form.[38]

There was something tangibly exciting about Dyos and Wolff's contention that the historian of the Victorian city had to consider its visual and symbolic form as well as its social structure – as seen in various book reviews and Dyos's personal correspondence.[39] This was, as Asa Briggs's essay on the Victorians' obsession with the statistical measurement of urban phenomena clearly establishes, a recognition that '[t]he world of Victorian cities was fragmented, intricate, eclectic, messy; and no single approach to their understanding provides us with all the right questions and answers or leads us to all the right available evidence'.[40] It pointed towards a new emphasis on cultural attitudes towards cities more generally, both the idea that the city was the largest art form of the nineteenth century, and, equally, the way that the city engendered all the hopes and fears of contemporary society.

The 1980s and 1990s saw an important shift in the field of urban history with the influence of the linguistic turn in history as a whole and the growing interest of urban historians in interrogating the different ways that urban culture is historically transmitted under the postmodern condition. This turn was in part an epistemological reaction to the social scientific approaches to studying the past, especially the Marxist tradition, which prioritized economic conditions as the driving variable behind historical change. It necessitated moving away from macro-level analyses of the past to prioritizing the multiple historical experiences; or, more succinctly, to study the multiple narratives of the past rather than one single meta-narrative. Calling for more micro histories of a particular place, and interrogating identity from multiple perspectives other than simply class (gender, sexuality, race and ethnicity, for example), this 'new cultural history' reflected an understanding that social reality and the categories coined to explain it were discursively constructed through language and that research could only ever produce a representation of that reality. It also indicated that there was no single structural explanation for urbanization, urban change or patterns of urban behaviour. Culture was subsequently given centre stage in explaining historical change and in moving away from meta-narratives of historical change, as we shall see in later chapters (see especially chapters 2, 3 and 5).

What this shift to cultural analysis meant, in practice, has been up for debate ever since. Some commentators, including Timothy Gilfoyle, claim that the presence of multiple narratives and conflicting interpretations has created 'interpretive confusion' within the field. He cites the example of the historiography on the World's Columbian Exposition of 1893 in Chicago, which, while it was once seen as a fairly straightforward example of physical planning and neoclassical architecture, is now 'an interpretive smorgasbord' of competing viewpoints:

> For urban historians, the Fair represents a metaphor for elite and plebeian values, a symbol of leisure and commercial cultures, the industrial city at its apogee, the physical embodiment of racial, ethnic, class and gender conflict, the beginning and the end of nineteenth-century planning, and the very essence of nineteenth-century American nationalism.[41]

There has subsequently been a growing tendency to narrow the interpretive lens on to the micro-scale case study with its shorter time span, which has arguably created what Stuart Blumin describes as 'temporal blindness' to the bigger picture of the place-in-context.[42]

Gilfoyle also concedes that this convergence of architectural, social and cultural history has opened up new vistas for scrutiny which have subsequently enriched research. These include the history of leisure, workplace culture, gender relations and domestic cultures, migrant and ethnic cultural identities, and the materiality of built landscapes. He cites the skyscraper as an embodiment of varied cultural meanings and social impacts: whereas skyscrapers littered the skyline of turn-of-the-twentieth-century New York, representing the drive for wealth and prestige there, in Boston and Chicago skyscraper construction was frustrated by the strict height restrictions to imitate the aesthetics of a European skyline. Moreover, given early skyscrapers' association with the newspaper and insurance industries, they were also, as Mona Domosh shows, material expressions of firms' commercial identities, of individual prestige and corporate power. New York's commercial elite, in particular, built high to express their individual status as well as their city's claims to be the 'capital of capitalism'. Technology, money and cultural sensibilities were thereby intermixed in order to generate localized responses towards a modern style of building.[43]

This cultural turn has undeniably gone hand in hand with a resurgence in scholarly organization, arguably to counteract a trend towards fragmentation within the field. When the *Urban History Yearbook* was relaunched in 1992 as *Urban History*, its editor Richard Rodger warned against scholarly fragmentation, as researchers brought their own 'distinctive tools and analytical concepts' to their studies, and increasingly broke off into specialist subgroups. The re-formation of the Urban History Group (UHG) in Britain in the 1990s, after a decade in abeyance, was one attempt to counteract this. Temporal fragmentation, between medieval, early modern and modern urban history, added another layer of complexity to the field. The Pre-Modern Towns Group, for example, has met since 1978 to discuss the historical study of towns in Britain and Europe from the early medieval period to the eighteenth century. *Urban History*, with its increased frequency of publication would, it was anticipated, provide a forum for discussion and research, thereby giving the field greater structure and clarity. Moreover, the continued publication of monographs and edited collections, especially those appearing in relevant book series, has given the field a renewed thematic coherence.[44]

The formation of learned societies since the late 1980s has similarly brought form to the networks of practising urban historians, and counteracted this trend towards fragmentation. National groups of urban historians have appeared in Britain, France, Germany, Italy, the Netherlands, the United States and elsewhere, while the European Association for Urban History (EAUH) has provided a multinational platform for urban historians since 1992. The practice of disciplinary elasticity is maintained through revolving conference themes, informal 'membership' (neither the EAUH or the UHG levy subscription fees or maintain membership lists, preferring to consider membership a reflection of one's continued participation at conferences) and a stress on collaborative organization (especially with the EAUH's preference for session organizers to work in different countries/universities). While aspects of the cultural experience of urban life have been recurring features of these societies' recent conferences, the round-table discussions frequently return to fundamental questions about the relationship between the experiential nature of life and the framing issues of urban economies, social identities and administration; the city rightly continues to be scrutinized in its totality.

An 'Urban Turn' Eastwards

We have so far concentrated on the rise and evolution of urban history in Western Europe and North America. While there has been a longer-term interest in the urban history of the developing world, not least in countries where the field was influenced by developments in Anglo-American urban history (South Africa and Canada, for instance),[45] the more recent past has seen a sustained growth in scholarly interest in the urban experience in countries undergoing intensive urbanization. Writing in 2002, for example, Gyan Prakash identified 'a noticeable surge' in interest in cities and city life in India. A rapid increase in the number of towns and cities – according to the 2011 census there are forty-six Indian cities with populations exceeding 1 million people – alongside the growing size of the country's urban population with over a third of the country's 1.21 billion population now living in urban areas, has obviously created many difficulties with enormous inequalities between those who relocate to the cities for casual employment, and the new Indian elite which enjoys growing political and economic opportunities.[46]

Prakash cites the activities of the Mumbai Studies Group, formed in 2000, as an example of the fusion of urban activism and scholarship from architects, journalists, cultural practitioners, anthropologists and historians alike, coming together to relocate India's modern history away from its rural roots on to a post-nationalist landscape where the politics of neoliberalism and globalization predominates.[47] This 'urban turn', as it has been labelled, has permeated Indian and South Asian historical scholarship ever since. This is particularly the case with Mumbai (formerly Bombay), the premier city of colonial and post-colonial India, which has attracted considerable interest in tracing its awesome growth from an archipelago of seven fishing islands into the sprawling megalopolis that is contemporary Mumbai, covering an area of over 4,000 square kilometres and with a population of more than 18 million inhabitants. It is a city, as Prashant Kidambi describes it, of 'staggering contrasts' between rich and poor:

> On the one hand, a vast majority of its population lives and works in abysmal conditions, densely packed into the city's teeming "slums," making a precarious living in the so-called informal sector. On the other hand, its affluent elites pursue lifestyles of calculated extravagance, fit to rival their counterparts in London or New York. Economic liberalization and "globalization" have only served to accentuate the startling iniquities between its "slumdogs" and its "millionaires."[48]

The contrasts between rich and poor in postcolonial cities have, inevitably, attracted considerable attention from urban historians as well as novelists and film-makers. This 'urban turn' is, then, a turn towards understanding the longer-term origins and escalation of social and economic inequalities within postcolonial urban societies, but is equally embedded in the cultural approaches outlined earlier. For example, Matthew Gandy has examined the ways that social inequalities in large postcolonial cities persistently manifest themselves through the material culture of technology, planning and engineering. Even though Mumbai bears the socio-technological and spatial imprints of modern civil engineering through its late Victorian water network, the city's slums lack basic sanitation or clean water and the poor suffer from high infant mortality rates and waterborne diseases. One author writes how severe weather events often leave the gutters and drains of the poor districts clogged up with the human waste of the rich. Indeed, the city's municipal water supply system, which transports nearly 3,000 million litres of water a day from the surrounding jungles, lakes and mountains of the state of Maharashtra, fails to meet the city's needs and businesses and residents alike are forced to rely upon old wells and boreholes scattered across the city, as well as private tanks and illegal connections.[49]

India's 'urban turn' is representative of a wider geographical awakening of interest in towns and cities in the developing world. Original research is being published about histories of urban life across hitherto under-studied regions, including Latin America, Africa, Eastern Europe and the Middle East, and is challenging old assumptions about urban form and development there.[50] Recent special issues of the *Journal of Urban History* and *Urban History* identify a similar 'urban turn' in Chinese historical studies, especially in the West, which has built on the early foundations laid by G. William Skinner and others. The opening of archives in the People's Republic of China (PRC) stimulated research into the country's urban history from within the PRC itself as well as from overseas. This efflorescence of interest reflects the country's emergence as an urban nation in the post-Mao era, in which more than half of the country's population of 1.355 billion now live in cities. The growing popularity of urban history has been accompanied by a flourishing interest in contemporary urban studies in the PRC and there is evidence that Chinese urban history is similarly interdisciplinary in its methodological and theoretical approaches.[51]

Whereas the earliest scholarly interest was in market towns in Ming- (1368–1644) and Qing- (1644–1911) era China, there has been a growing interest more recently in the last years of the Qing dynasty and the Republican era (c.1840–1949) when Chinese culture came into more regular contact with the new, Western-influenced urban culture developing in the foreign-run concessionaries of treaty ports such as Shanghai, Nanking and Tianjin. As Rana Mitter writes, 'The treaty port cities, and in particular Shanghai, created a particular type of imperial modernity that sometimes seemed to suspend the reality that the cities were squarely in Chinese territory, inhabited mostly by Chinese.' Mitter also cites examples of 'outward-looking' modernity, such as the writer

Shi Zhecun, 'who wandered around the bookstores of the International Settlement and the coffee shops of the French Concession, living a Parisian Left Bank lifestyle at one remove.'[52]

Other historians have examined the ways that Western and native Chinese cultures have mixed during this period. Ruth Rogaski, for example, traces the way that Western understandings of health and disease mixed with the traditional Chinese meaning of hygiene (*weisheng*) as an all-encompassing way of life. Thus, *weisheng's* traditional association with regimens of diet, meditation and self-medication was conflated with the arrival of imperial state power and the scientific and racialized standards of cleanliness and hygiene to produce a hybridized version of 'hygienic modernity' in treaty-port Tianjin. China's global awakening from its national subjugation was, for Rogaski then, centred on the practice of *weisheng*, that is, the medicalization of China's problems, which is why Tianjin was the first Chinese city to have its own native-administered municipal department of health (1902).[53]

Shanghai, the country's largest city with a population of 19 million, attracts especial interest from both contemporary scholars and historians interested in accounting for its status as a global megacity. Historical studies of the city's municipal administration, police and street culture reflect its reputation as a hotbed for new cultural forms. Shanghai's urban elite, like so many others in this period, developed its own identity fuelled by a rich financial and commercial culture, regulated by an organized body of municipal officials, and offering an eclectic mixture of traditional and modern attractions to the floods of visitors. These included Western attractions and novelties such as foreign films, exposed public toilets, dancing halls and jazz music, which functioned alongside long-established cultural traditions or reworked versions of these, such as vernacular architecture, opera, and a local literature and film culture.[54] This example is illustrative of the convergence of themes between Chinese and Western urban history, particularly around urban modernization, municipal politics, material culture and everyday life, reflecting the tensions and contradictions of modernity with Chinese social and cultural traditions.

Urban history has taken a number of conceptual, methodological and geographical 'turns' as the field has evolved and become more organized during the twentieth century. It is geographically richer and thematically and theoretically denser than the urban history practised in the 1950s; it draws upon an ever widening range of disciplines and approaches to explain the urban past; whilst researchers benefit from having access to more numerous outlets for disseminating their research. This includes e-publishing, multimedia publishing (through well-established outlets such as *Urban History*), edited electronic discussion lists like H-Urban, personal blogging and social media like Twitter, as well as a widening number of national and international conferences in urban history, planning and architectural history, social and economic history, environmental history and historical geography to name but a few.

Yet in other ways it is similar to the urban history practised in the early to mid-twentieth century: crucially the field rightly remains committed to charting the history of urbanization and the contextualized history of towns and cities in their totality. It is also a field populated by outward-looking practitioners, ever willing to communicate their research with urban activists, journalists and policymakers; it continues to look for historical explanations for the current urban condition – both as a global condition but also seeking the local circumstances of growth and decline. This is because its practitioners continue to sit comfortably at the intersection of the humanities and social sciences, recognizing that interdisciplinarity is more fertile and widens the potential field of impact for original research.

2
Cities, Spaces and Identities

A growing trend in the London and New York housing markets has seen upmarket apartment blocks built for high-income groups, incorporating affordable homes for poorer residents (including single-parent families, the elderly, and low-paid ethnic minorities) in order to secure planning permission. Yet this has not led to greater social integration between rich and poor; quite the opposite in fact. The apartment blocks have in-built segregated spaces, with separate entrances, storage spaces, rubbish disposal facilities and even separate postal deliveries, on the grounds that 'the two social strata don't have to meet'. Access to the affordable housing is via 'poor doors' in darkly lit side alleyways, whereas the wealthy residents enter via staffed hotel-style lobby areas.[1]

Such an example reveals how inner-city residential segregation extends to the micro-scale, in this case to the same block of apartments. This is not new, of course: segregation by income and status dictated which floor families lived on in the tenements of Edinburgh's Old Town before its great fire of 1824, or in Vienna's apartment blocks and Mexico City's *vecindades*, amongst numerous other examples. There has also been, as the North American scholarship demonstrates, long-standing segregation on grounds of ethnicity and race. But this example does illustrate how one social group's spatial choices are inextricably linked to another's, and how their identities are rooted in their ability to make decisions about where they want to live. Decisions about housing are never made in a vacuum; neither are identities. Social identities are constructed and enacted within space, acting upon the design and usage of that space, and involve the actions of property developers, financiers, governments, landlords and residents themselves.

This example is also the tip of an enormous iceberg. The historiography on the morphology of cities reveals a sustained interest in the relationship between space and identity since at least the 1960s and, specifically, the creation of spatially segregated cities.[2] This has traditionally been the case in the urban historiography of the English-speaking world, but it has also extended more widely than this. As we shall see in this chapter, urban historians have examined the ways in which key spaces within cities (focusing here on the residential spaces of high- and low-income social groups in the form of the suburb and the slum) are formed in parallel with the construction and negotiation of social identities; they have subsequently traced changing understandings of both identity and space over time. As Simon Gunn eloquently puts it, 'Space is an active element in the constitution of social identities.' Since social identities are formed historically in and from spatial reorganizations, it follows that 'social identities are frequently forged in conflicts over the boundaries, ownership and meaning of places'.[3] The city itself is, therefore, an active participant in historical change.

Whereas class has traditionally been the over-arching social identity examined in Western historiography, the more recent cultural turn has generated enormous interest in less traditional forms of identity and their relationship to space, specifically gender, sexuality, race and ethnicity. North American scholarship, in particular, strongly reflects this shifting focus on to 'ethno-cultural' approaches towards the history of immigration and social mobility.[4] Drawing upon theoretical work in anthropology and geography, urban historians now broadly agree that cities and spaces are as much 'landscapes of the mind' as social and physical environments. Yet there also remains a well-established consensus that the housing choices of different groups reflect the innate social and economic inequalities rooted within urban capitalistic society. Research into cities in formerly colonial societies has revealed the complex interplay of ethnic, gendered, and class-based identities in generating what Brodwyn Fischer calls a sense of 'insecure permanence' to mark the social divide between rich and poor in the developing world.[5] As we shall see, the most rewarding studies of socio-spatial segregation have utilized a comparative framework, either exploring identity formation in different towns and cities, or across temporal boundaries in the same place; or they have examined the ways in which multiple identities have intersected in the same place through a dual emphasis on the material and cultural experiences of urban life.

Class, Space and the Suburban Ideal

Urban historians have, since the 1960s, examined the growing pace and intensity of socio-spatial segregation through patterns of residence, mobility and interaction, with particular reference to the urban-industrializing era of the eighteenth and nineteenth centuries. The suburb, as old as the city itself, has attracted voluminous and sustained interest to the extent that it has spawned a subfield of 'suburban studies' with its own anthologies, special issues of periodicals and review articles.[6] The two defining histories of suburbanization were by H. J. Dyos on Camberwell (South London) and Sam Bass Warner, Jr, on Boston (Massachusetts), both of which concluded that nineteenth-century economic, social and technological changes generated a standard type of urban development in the form of the suburb, defined by Dyos as 'a decentralized part of a city with which it is inseparably linked by certain economic and social ties'.[7] While we now find Dyos's definition limited, not least for its neglect of cultural perceptions of suburbia, his emphasis on the interconnectedness between the suburb and its parent city adhered to the 'containing context' model of urban history outlined in the previous chapter. Moreover, since both studies were published in the early 1960s, during a period of heightened debate about the future of the city, both used their cases, as revealed in correspondence in the Dyos Collection, to argue in favour of practical urban planning, advocating the value of learning from past experiences as 'a necessity for present demands'.[8]

Although both recognized the development of space as integral to suburbanization, they tended to see geographical patterns of segregation as reflecting society in class terms only. Warner's study was based on the premise that suburbanization was a middle-class phenomenon in which only affluent families could afford the exclusivity of the suburban home, condemning the working classes to remain in central areas close to work. He writes how, by 1900, Boston had become 'a city divided' between an inner city of work and low-income housing and an outer city of middle- and upper-income residences. Dyos, meanwhile, exposed the changing socio-economic composition of Victorian Camberwell, charting the development and growth of 'suburban slum' districts from the mid-nineteenth century through a process of 'infilling', sub-leasing and overcrowding. Thus, 'black spots' noted by cramped houses, lower-class residents (he cites the 'clannish Irish' inhabiting one street) and noxious industries (glue and linoleum factories, for example) appeared in parts of Camberwell by mid-century to give the area 'both the odours and the society of the authentic slum'. These areas were subsequently physically sealed off by the entry of the railway and the building of a viaduct, which further exacerbated the slum-like conditions.[9]

Both studies were hugely influential over later research, published in the 1970s and 1980s, on the morphology of the modern city. Yet this new generation of scholars came to conflicting conclusions about the timing of suburbanization. In Britain, David Ward argued that residential segregation was fairly insignificant until late in the nineteenth century for all but the wealthiest groups, while David Cannadine contended that rapid population growth, landownership and the emergence of a middle class with sharply defined cultural values led to clear residential segregation by mid-century. The differences largely stemmed from the selection of case studies. Whereas the fast-growing industrial towns of Birmingham and Manchester exhibited clear socio-spatial patterns of residential segregation by the 1840s, with the rich increasingly living at the periphery and the poor left huddled in the centre, smaller-sized towns like Chorley, Exeter and Lincoln exhibited a reverse position. Ward notes that these towns shared similarities with the sociologist Gideon Sjoberg's pre-industrial model of a city, where the patrician elite of land-owners, aristocracy and civic leaders dwelt at the centre in large properties, while the poor congregated at the periphery in densely packed areas; the majority in between tended to live in areas based on ethnicity, family and occupation ties rather than socio-economic status. Critics of Sjoberg, however, argue that, notwithstanding the specific problems with the 'pre-industrial' model, it undervalues a developmen-tal model of the city that takes into account 'a whole series of changes, each engendering the next and spread over a much longer period', creating an artificial divide between the 'pre-industrial', 'proto-industrial' and 'industrial' periods. A more empirically nuanced perspective is what is required, according to Peter Burke, and this is what Ward aims at in his important article.[10]

Kenneth Jackson, on the other hand, cites the advent of mass transport in the second half of the nineteenth century and the first half of the twentieth as fundamentally changing the spatial layout of the city, ushering in a new era of segre-gation based on class and income, especially in North America. As the metropolitan area increasingly expanded outwards in a centrifugal fashion, cheap land around the fringe was developed into exclusive higher-income suburbs, the residents of which travelled into the city for work by railroad/tram (first horse-drawn, then steam and, finally, from the 1890s, electric) or, in the larger cities, railway and, later, the motor car. Jackson cites the importance of the avail-ability of transport options in explaining the decision taken by the American middle class to move into the suburbs, which, aided by heavy state subsidies and cheap mortgages (especially following the National Housing Act of 1934), made the dream of a suburban home a socio-economic reality for 'almost all white, middle-income families'. To support his argument, Jackson leans heavily on the Burgess model of urban development in explaining the rise of the 'automobile suburb' in the twentieth century with its lower density, larger lot size and culture of ranch-style houses, which set the North American suburb apart from anything else in the urban world. This was coupled with the emergence of a new 'drive-in culture' with its own vernacular – the interstate highway system, motel, gasoline station, drive-in cinema and shopping centre.[11]

Burgess's link between mass transportation and suburbanization is weakened when applied to the British case, where new areas of attractive middle-class housing had developed since Georgian times at least – these included the Blythswood estate in Glasgow, the Park and Little Woodhouse estates in Leeds, and Edinburgh's New Town. Many of these early walking suburbs were built in the western parts of the existing built-up area, away from the harmful effects of polluting smoke, which was carried away by prevailing south-westerly winds. However, because of their fairly central location, these proto-suburbs were quickly surrounded by lower-middle-class and working-class developments as industrialization and urbanization gathered pace during the second and third decades of the century. This in turn brought its own concomitant problems with smoke, higher densities and unattractive housing, which forced the middle class to relocate again.[12] Thus began what David Cannadine calls 'the golden years of exclusive, middle-class suburbia', from 1820 to 1870, in which neighbouring villages and undeveloped land a few miles from urban centres was colonized, as at Headingley and Chapeltown in Leeds, while exclusive middle-class neighbourhoods were developed by landowning families like the Calthorpes at Edgbaston, on the south-western side of Birmingham, or the Butes at Cardiff. These suburbs were connected to the centre by private horse-drawn transport and pre-date the mass transportation era identified by adherents to the Burgess model; in fact, the arrival of mass transit forms helps to account for the growing subdivision of these neighbourhoods with the arrival of the lower middle class and working classes in the period 1870–1914, which leaves Cannadine to conclude that mass transportation actually threatened, rather than strengthened, the exclusivity of middle-class suburbs.[13]

What made North America such fertile breeding ground for suburbanization, Jackson argues, was that its national culture was founded on a general dislike of urban life. This fear was exacerbated by massive and sustained population growth during the nineteenth century, including unprecedented immigration of African-Americans from the South, which incentivized white flight to the suburbs and was accompanied by the provision of improved services. Economic factors were also important for explaining the North American suburban dream, notably higher per capita wealth, the existence of inexpensive land and transport options, state subsidies for speculative development, and the widespread adoption of the inexpensive balloon-frame house, but, Jackson insists, socio-spatial segregation in North America was largely driven by an interplay of class-based, racial and ethnic identities.[14]

The suburban ideal was not, however, wholly exceptional to North America. Graeme Davison traces its deep roots into Australia's colonial experience, where it was aggressively promoted by the country's founders and expressed the aspirations of the newly arrived immigrants, mostly from Britain. In many ways the Australian suburb was similar to that which developed in the British metropole: it provided 'a zone of exclusively bourgeois residence' for the wealthy to enjoy a rural domesticated lifestyle away from the clamour of the city. What distinguished it from its British counterparts, however, was 'the swiftness with which the ideal was diffused and the low barriers that colonial society presented to its attainment'. Sydney, Hobart, Perth, Melbourne and Adelaide were all founded as low-density, low-rise suburban cities within a few years of each other; they subsequently enjoyed lower population densities than British or even many North American cities outside of the Midwest. Australian suburbs, then, represented the last stage in a long journey for many working-class emigrants whose travels had started in a village or provincial town in Britain and who were keen to aspire to an Anglicized middle-class way of life intermixed with respectable working-class traditions of self-help and cooperation.[15]

As Davison's conclusions indicate, suburbs never solely harnessed an exclusive middle-class domestic culture. Comparative and longitudinal approaches have debunked the myth that there was an intrinsic link between middle-class society and suburbia, identifying the enormous diversity of forms that have existed: these include white working-class suburbs, immigrant suburbs and ethnically diverse suburbs, as well as planned and unplanned suburbs. Richard Lawton,

Richard Dennis and Colin Pooley used published census tabulations to paint a more complex spatial organization of society in mid-nineteenth-century Liverpool, segregated along lines of socio-economic, family, and ethnic or migrant status. High levels of intra-urban migration further reveal the changing complexities of residential segregation and social identity formation over time. Thriving proto-industrial suburbs have been traced across medieval English cities like Coventry. A recent study of the planning of Latin America's capital cities reveals a mixed range of influences – from Haussmann-era Paris to British garden cities to North America's city beautiful – mixed with localized traditions to create varied landscapes in cities ranging from Buenos Aires to San José do Costa Rica. Post-Second World War European cities like Paris, Berlin, Milan and Stockholm embraced high-rise, high-density suburbs to house low-income tenants, such as the *banlieues* outside Paris, while the rich continued to live around the historic city centres, often in high-rise apartments too. Britain also experienced a proliferation of suburban housing estates during the interwar period and, after the Second World War, mass-produced council housing estates to house the working classes.[16]

In an excellent study, Richard Harris and Robert Lewis demonstrate remarkable levels of 'segregated diversity' in the composition and function of North American and Canadian suburbs during the first half of the twentieth century. They trace the decentralization of employment and residential patterns across cities with diverse socio-economic bases (Montreal, Toronto, Chicago and Los Angeles) and conclude that 'industrial suburbanization' involved the relocation of offices, stores and factories, as well as the widespread suburbanization of workers and immigrants to the periphery, thereby producing socially diverse suburbs. 'Certainly,' they write, 'no general contrast can be made between city and suburb in terms of social class.' And contemporaries knew this: older, prosperous enclaves persisted in inner cities, such as Chestnut Hill in Philadelphia and Montreal's New Town, while rich and poor lived cheek-by-jowl in Chicago's Near North. Similar diversity existed in the suburbs, with Chicago having 23 suburbs by 1940 with populations greater than 10,000. Of these, 9 had rents below the metropolitan average, and only 8 enjoyed rents that were exclusive. In Toronto, Harris has shown how blue-collar suburbs, numbering some tens of thousands in population, developed during the early 1920s around the nuclear single-family house, albeit often with lodgers to supplement the family income. There was similar complexity in the ethnic and racial composition of the suburbs, with many lower-income industrial suburbs containing white immigrants in cities like Philadelphia and Detroit by 1920, while black suburbanites also used the additional domestic space to generate extra income by taking in lodgers or offering laundry services.[17]

Suburbia as Gendered Space

The majority of studies cited thus far pay scant attention to the families that relocated to suburbia. Women, in particular, were absent from early studies, which is unsurprising given the relatively recent development of women's history in the 1970s and 1980s. Since then, there has been a convergence between women's and gender history, which has left its mark on urban history. There is also growing interest in the history of masculinity in cities, paying particular attention to the ways that men construct and manage urban spaces, in the private as well as the public domains, to reflect a hegemonic understanding of masculinity as middle class, white and heterosexual. This broad literature has subsequently influenced how gender ideologies of masculinity and femininity are inextricably linked to the processes of urbanization and suburbanization, but more research clearly needs to be done.[18]

Given that Anglo-American historians have long agreed that the separation of the gender order into defined spheres of public (male predominantly) and domestic (female *and* male) spaces and roles was a unifying component of middle-class ideology, the relationship between masculinity and femininity has obviously played a significant role in shaping suburban domestic space. Catherine Hall and Leonore Davidoff demonstrate how gender played a formative role in structuring provincial urban middle-class culture in England, marked by the ideology of domesticity and separate spheres, in the late eighteenth and early nineteenth centuries. Middle-class women were seen as carriers of morality whose domestic role was to sustain a respectable, gentrified lifestyle for their family, while men were released from such moral restraints in order to participate in the public world of work and politics.[19]

This suburban ideal of privacy and domesticity developed, then, as a masculine ethos informed by Christian evangelicalism: men designed and built the houses; they even planned the internal division of space in order to reaffirm traditional gender roles. Thus, the *house*wife was associated with the kitchen and the nursery (alongside her female servants), while the husband's domestic role was limited to maintaining household fixtures (the plumbing, for example), the garden, and space behind closed doors (dens, studies and garden sheds). The male builders of suburbia thus espoused their own version of feminized domesticity in which family and the sanctity of the home kept mothers and their children shielded from the dangers of city life; these were reinforced by the spread of codes of behaviour via periodicals and manuals aimed at middle-class women.[20]

This persistent gender ideology was subsequently influential in debates around the emergence of modern planning at the turn of the twentieth century. As women campaigned publicly for greater economic and political rights to the city, few dissenting voices could be heard within planning circles, largely because 'male professionals were *the* progressive response to the dark environmental era of the nineteenth century'. Planners like Patrick Geddes, Raymond Unwin and J. Horace McFarland worked comfortably within the ideology of separate spheres, and, through their adherence to the principles of the garden city and city beautiful movements, their interventions in the built environment 'reinforced ideals of domesticity, the separation of home and workplace, an ordering of space so that women could, first and foremost, fulfil their roles as wives and mothers in a world separated from that of men'. As late as the 1940s, the most influential propagandists on post-war reconstruction continued to espouse an old-fashioned understanding of gender identity despite women's important contributions to the economy and society in successive wars.[21]

Gender stereotypes continued to shape the construction and remodelling of space during the twentieth century, then, and not merely in middle-class enclaves. The dormitory town of Levittown, New York, which was originally designed to house returning GI servicemen and their families after the Second World War, provides a good illustration of this. Jackson narrates the story from the viewpoint of the builders, Levitt and Son, who encouraged a generation of baby boomers to own their own homes. Sited 25 miles east of Manhattan, Levittown was the largest private housing project in US history, with 17,400 mass-produced emergency houses constructed with an eye on speed and efficiency: the builders used pre-cut lumber and nails, and built them on concrete slabs. Each 'box house' was architecturally uniform according to a simple plan: with a living room situated at the back of the house overlooking the back yard, two bedrooms, and a kitchen situated at the front so that mothers could watch their children playing from kitchen windows while they prepared meals and washed clothes. Levittown was, therefore, built according to stereotypical gendered understandings of family dynamics – domesticity, privacy and conformity – and not merely to save on building costs.[22]

More recently, Barbara Kelly argues that, instead of viewing Levittown as an attempt by builders and government officials to impose middle-class values on a working-class community, residents actively reshaped their own environment to produce a community of individualized homes, albeit one that conformed to the expectations of a suburban domestic lifestyle. They did this by converting unfinished attics into new bedrooms, and re-dividing internal space to create dining rooms, dens, storage rooms and 'granny flats'. Kelly traces these physical modifications on to family life cycles to produce a 'social morphology' of Levittown: events such as the arrival of new babies, adolescence and ageing grandparents necessitated changes to the spatial layout of the house. The Levittown homeowner, then, was a 'co-producer' in the housing market, which meant that women also played a key role in reshaping the local environment, and in transforming houses into homes.[23]

The late twentieth and early twenty-first centuries, too, witnessed a challenge to the male breadwinner nuclear family, with the rise of single-parent, blended, lesbian and gay families across cities, particularly in the West. This is as applicable to suburbia as it is to the inner city and further questions our understandings of space there. Thus, Veronica Strong-Boag et al. contend that, since these non-traditional suburbanites tend to be '[m]arginalized by dominant discourses of "the family", they may well experience suburban space differently and encounter special isolation and difficulty'.[24] Yet for all this we know little about the experience of homosexuals living in suburbia, particularly because heterosexuality has historically been the normative sexuality there, which has inevitably meant that suburbanite gays and lesbians have had to 'pass' as heterosexual. Rather, historians have tended to map 'gay territories' in major Western inner-city areas like the Castro in San Francisco, Greenwich Village in New York, and Darlinghurst in Sydney, because they are more visible and have their own defined cultural traditions (see chapter 5).[25]

In recent years sociologists have tracked the creation of linked gay suburban communities through societies such as the South Western Area Gays and Lesbians (SWAGLS) in western Sydney, as well as everyday relationships that distinguish suburban gay from inner-city gay identities. As Stephen Hodge argues in relation to late twentieth-century western Sydney, the gay suburban home has become a place where bridges can be built between heterosexual and homosexual communities, to foster better understandings of 'different' social groups, and where the construction of sexual identities is blurred with class, ethnicity and family, rather than maintaining simplified gay (inner-city) and 'non-gay' (suburban) spaces. In this case, western Sydney as a cultural space exists as much in homosexual identities and imaginations as in the heterosexual mind, while suburban gay identity draws upon the powerful suburban ideal expressed through the individual pursuit for privacy, space and domesticity.[26]

Poverty, Ethnicity and Gender in the Making of the 'Slum'

The most commonly studied social group in urban historiography has been the 'urban poor'. While the appellation 'poor' has traditionally been taken to be a measure of poverty, multiple studies have stressed the plurality of individuals who constitute this social category: they range from mill and factory workers to casually employed labourers, hawkers, street vendors and pedlars, market sellers, domestic servants and child workers. They are connected by the informality and irregularity of their work, their historic lack of labour rights, high rates of turnover in the labour market, low pay and poor opportunities for social mobility. The vast majority were rural migrants who moved to cities to find work; the irregular pattern of employment meant that they often retained their rural connections, rather than permanently settling in the cities, which, as James Ferguson illustrates in his study of miners in Zambia's Copperbelt region, generated difficulties in assimilating into urban society. Moreover, as Nandini Gooptu has demonstrated, 'urban poor' is itself an elite construct designed to make sense of 'a footloose and volatile mass' who threatened 'the moral and social well-being of "respectable" people'. This 'outcast' discourse has been traced to the writings and public speeches of a variety of educated actors, including journalists, social reformers and politicians across the nineteenth and twentieth centuries in cities ranging from Bombay to London and Lusaka to Paris.[27]

Space is integral to the formation of identities for the 'urban poor' because of the historic relationship between work, home and leisure for the labouring classes, particularly under the time-and-labour-discipline culture generated by urban-industrial capitalism. Time and space were closely connected in shaping working-class identities in the manufacturing town: the working day was bound by time, which was carefully measured and monitored in the workplace, and workers were disciplined if they were late for work. Clocks dominated the facades of factories, town halls, schools and churches to remind workers of the importance of being time-disciplined. The relationship between time, space and identity, then, was particularly significant for the 'urban poor' both in terms of their lack of control over their everyday lives and elite perceptions of how much control they should be subjected to within the workplace.[28]

This level of control extended outside the workplace into the poor's limited residential choices. Unable to pay high rents, the poor have historically been forced into a low standard of rental housing, always in overcrowded conditions as near as possible to work to reduce the cost and time of commuting; though increasingly, particularly in cities in the developing world, they are being forced to relocate to the outskirts, often outside their formal legal boundaries and without access to basic municipal services like drainage, clean water and electricity. The subsequent discovery of 'slums', as they are historically known, has generated a uniform approach and derogatory language that is used to describe, analyse, condemn and 'reform' the habitats and culture of the slum-dwellers. Urban historians from Dyos onwards have focused on a variety of primary sources – including newspaper accounts, the reports of health officials, municipal and legal records, and, to a lesser extent, the accounts of the urban poor themselves – to give physical form to the slum and place it in the wider system of urban capitalism. Empirical research reveals how the slum and the suburb, as 'real' places, have been historically connected in this system of capitalist exploitation. After all, argued Dyos, Reeder and Rodger, the middle-class 'slum landlord' often funded his suburban home from the profits he made from poor tenants.[29]

More recently, a revisionist literature has shifted focus away from the conditions within the slum to studying its representation within popular discourse. Most significantly, in his comparative account of the representation of slum literature in late Victorian Birmingham, New York and Sydney, Alan Mayne argues that when we read accounts of the slum conditions of the 'urban poor', we are presented with 'highly stylized sets rather than locations, one dimensional types rather than people, and prepared scripts rather than spontaneous social exchanges'. Slums are as much cultural artefacts and constructions of the journalistic imagination and the prejudices of municipal authorities as they are popular reflections of the limited life choices available to poor city residents. This view certainly reveals how the politically charged term 'slum' has different historical, linguistic and cultural meanings in different countries, tinged with a variety of emotions, including fear, disgust, shame, nostalgia and celebration of community: wynds, rookeries, *bidonvilles*, ghettos, *colonias populares*, *barriadas*, *campaneto*, *musseques*, *favelas*, etc. What links them together is a broader understanding that they are constructed within the 'bourgeois imagination' in order to condense 'complex spatial forms and social conditions into readily comprehensible images of deprivation and social pathology'.[30]

The slum is also a product of the urban poor's lives and their everyday struggles to adapt to a fast-growing urban society. This is particularly highlighted by comparative studies, which reveal important distinctions between the standards of housing, the options available to slum-dwellers, and the cultural and political significance of slum districts: for instance, the distinctions between Rio de Janeiro's and São Paulo's *cortiços* (large houses divided into small rooms) and *favelas* (autonomous self-built neighbourhoods). External factors and socio-political crises are also significant: years of destructive civil war across the Congo and Angola since decolonization, coupled with outdated or irrelevant planning statutes, have forced hundreds of thousands of people to move into squalid and overcrowded shanty towns in the capitals of Brazzaville and Luanda.[31]

There are even shades of social mobility within slums, as Hanchao Lu has shown in his captivating study of the different types of slum-dwelling in Shanghai's shantytowns between the 1920s and 1940s. By comparing the city's different slums over time, Lu shows how the wider socio-economic and political context of the period had significant bearing on the standard of house construction and the status attached to particular building types. Thus, the early *penghu* straw shacks that went up in the Yaoshuilong settlement alongside Suzhou Creek, despite their flimsy construction and mud floors, were, for their residents at least, a step above the emergency "trash dump" shacks built at Fangualong during the Sino–Japanese War (1937–45) or the *shuishang gelou* ('loft on the water') shacks built *on* the water in the Zhaojiabang slum that sprung up during the Civil War (1946–9). Armed conflict, mixed with the general deterioration of the rural economy, brought an influx of rural migrants into the city, transformed existing spaces, found new uses for old spaces, and forced the weakest and most vulnerable groups into a moveable residential space with awful health risks when, on rainy days, 'the so-called "lofts *on* the water" became "lofts *in* the water"'.[32]

We have already seen how a suburb could develop slum-like properties through intensive redevelopment, overcrowding and a lack of amenities. Some suburbs developed to house the urban poor to keep them away from the historic heartlands of the city centre, where the wealthy elite preferred to live, as was the case in Paris and Vienna, and where their inhabitants were described in terms of the 'Other' to the civilized groups living in the centre.[33] Other slums emerged because the urban poor were forced to relocate to irregular, informal and even illegal settlements on the urban fringe by councils which ruthlessly bulldozed inner-city districts of low-income housing inhabited by newly arrived migrants, as famously depicted by the 'Bulldozer Mayor', Ernest Uruchurtu, in 1960s Mexico City. Large-scale slum clearance in cities in the developing world during the second half of the twentieth century coincided with high-profile international events like sporting competitions and dignitary visits. In his engrossing book, *The Planet of Slums*, Mike Davis cites Manila as one such case where successive clearances between 1974 and 1976 displaced around 160,000 of the urban poor some 30 kilometres or more from their former homes, in order to create parade routes for the Miss Universe pageant (1974), the visit of US President Gerald Ford (1975), and the IMF-World Bank conference (1976). Even more brutally, 720,000 people were relocated in Seoul-Injon for the 1988 Olympic Games, while a recent report claims that approximately 1.5 million Beijing residents were displaced due to Olympics-related redevelopment projects between 2000 and 2008 (about 14 per cent of the city's permanent population), in addition to the demolition of some of its 'villages-in-the-city' (*cheongzhongcun*) inhabited by temporary migrant renters.[34]

The removal of slum housing, as well as the subsequent relocation of the displaced, has always been politically charged, then, and is accompanied by elitist prejudices about the way that the poor live. Housing demand has invariably always exceeded supply, especially during periods of high urban in-migration. For example, Paris faced an acute housing shortage during the second half of the nineteenth century, which led to an increasing spatial division by class between the wealthy elites housed in spacious apartments in the western, inner *arrondisements*, paying high rents, and the poorer immigrants from the countryside who lived in heavily overcrowded eastern and outer districts. Socio-spatial segregation was, according to Harold Platt, documented in Parisians' individual liberty and the privileging of private property, which had been enshrined in French law since the 1789 revolution.[35]

Moreover, slum clearance programmes across the world have invariably created a disparity between the number of houses demolished and the number of new homes built for the displaced. The urban poor are often forced to relocate into existing overcrowded districts or, as is often the case in the developing world, build their own homes on vacant land, often far away from jobs and civic amenities. Baron Georges-Eugène Haussmann's redevelopment of Paris's city centre during the 1850s and 1860s displaced roughly 350,000 people, and culminated with the building of shantytowns around the city's suburbs comprised of illegal subdivisions, jerry-builds and lodging houses. A similar case existed in early twentieth-century Chicago and Detroit, where white residents used property law to create a bi-racial landscape of inequality by excluding African-American migrants from the South. A series of restrictive covenants and eviction orders were subsequently invoked by municipal councils and real-estate developers to force black migrants into high-density areas of the cities, while white 'slumlords' worsened housing conditions by subdividing apartments, using cardboard walls in some cases, and artificially raising rents. They also simultaneously failed to provide basic sanitation services: a 1917 study of Detroit's East Side District ghetto found 25 per cent of homes had only outside toilets, while many more had inside toilets located, without partition, either in a bedroom or in the kitchen. White middle- and working-class residents thus reconstructed their own social identities through 'a political culture of racism and corruption combined with the sanctity of property', and these were spatially reinforced through the subsequent 'piling up' of black migrants into ghetto districts.[36]

Colonial African cities were also subject to ethnic and class segregation, which played a decisive role in the formation of new social identities as well as reflecting Western racism. New urban quarters, such as the Hill Station suburb above

Freetown in Sierra Leone, or planned redevelopments of entire towns as at Lourenço Marques (Maputo), the capital city of Portuguese East Africa (Mozambique), created white-only enclaves on the grounds of fears about disease and miscegenation. The indigenous black population was, along with the white residents' refuse, expelled to the cities' out-skirts. As Vivian Bickford-Smith has shown, the ideology of 'racial separation' originated in Cape Town in the course of economic and social changes wrought by the mining revolu-tion in the Cape region during the final third of the nineteenth century. Cape Town society underwent revolutionary change, including segregation by colour and income, during a period of unprecedented industrialization, urbanization and immi-gration. This shaped an emerging white bourgeois *and* English identity, the adherents of which defined themselves in ethnic and racial as well as class terms, and, in so doing, defined the poor and the non-white population against their own criteria. This produced 'a racist discourse' within the Cape-tonian press and on the municipal council, particularly in categorizing the variety of non-white groups as 'Black Cape-tonians', who were subsequently scapegoated for many of the social ills of the fast-growing city. Not only were 'Black Capetonians' excluded from white-only residential areas of the city, but they were also prevented from entering certain restaurants and hotels, while the city's first privately owned roller-skating rink was opened in 1879, operating a policy of excluding all black people.[37]

Historical studies of Indian cities also illustrate the ethnic and class-driven discrepancies between housing reform and the lived reality of the urban poor. For example, it took a bubonic plague epidemic during the 1890s to compel India's colonial authorities to intervene in the provision of housing for Bombay's poor. By creating a City Improvement Trust in 1898, the authorities established a spatial link between poverty, ethnicity, caste and disease through insanitary housing. Similar cases existed in Calcutta, where an improve-ment trust was set up in 1911 following an earlier plague scare, and also in the larger towns of the United Provinces, where trusts were founded in the years after 1919 to clear 'plague spots' of overcrowded and insanitary housing. In all cases, the trustees, who were drawn from the cities' propertied elite, saw housing reform as an opportunity to both improve the working classes' morality and display their own benevolence. Prejudice was also linguistically constructed through popular and derogatory synonyms, such as 'poor-class people', 'inferior classes' and 'lower classes', which failed to differentiate between the casual poor and the respectable industrial workers. This culminated in a series of class- and caste-driven policies that targeted the poor's religious and social activities, as well as their living arrangements, on the assumption that the property-owning classes could socialize the poor while preserving forms of traditional communal life.[38]

Such a 'civilizing mission' reinforced the linkages between identity and space, not least when, because of escalating land values and the consequent competition for urban space, proposed rehousing projects threatened the harmony and exclusivity of existing middle-class areas. Examples included the appearance of self-built shanty huts on vacant land bordering a colonial civil servants' complex in interwar Kanpur. Following complaints from the property owners that the urban poor were using a plot of land adjacent to their bungalows as a public latrine, the trust intervened and removed the huts. Urban propertied elites regularly blocked the construction of tenements for the poor near their own areas in fear of diminished property values and moral anxieties about the possible spread of disease; these were themselves shaped by fears about class, racial degeneration and an incipient dislike of the urban poor.[39]

Socio-spatial segregation, then, was equally driven by property developers seeking to maximize profits from their investments. India's improvement trusts were, on the whole, disinclined to provide land for housing the displaced poor because they lacked a recurring income and preferred to cater for the residential needs of the middle class. Even when low-income estates were provided for the displaced poor, usually on trust-owned land on the edges of the city – as in the case of the *ahatas* (complexes of small houses in walled compounds built for the labouring population) in interwar Kanpur – these quickly degenerated into slums again because the trustees were unwilling to subject the house-builders and owners to building regulations or rent controls. Municipal building and sanitary codes similarly went unenforced in twentieth-century Rio, where they clashed with builders' financial interests. Where sanitary services like water supplies and public latrines were provided in low-income areas, this often pushed rents up beyond the reach of those whom they were supposed to house, which further solidified segregation because the poor were pushed further into the informal housing market. This 'served only to worsen the housing conditions of the poor' and, as Gooptu concludes, 'divided the town spatially more and more into areas for the rich or the middle classes and for the poor'.[40]

The provision of infrastructural services and people's everyday activities, including going to the toilet, also reflected the negotiation of social identities and their grounding in space. Whereas the rich have, in modern times, benefited from the provision of private water closets in their homes, the historical lack of public and private toilets in poor neighbourhoods has posed major challenges for all residents, particularly women, and is a reflection of their weak influence over powerful groups like property developers, water suppliers, and municipalities. In the Laini Saba district of Nairobi's Kibera slum (the largest urban slum in Africa), there were only ten working pit latrines for 40,000 residents in 1998, while in the city's Mathare 4A slum there were a miserly two public toilets to go around 28,000 people. Residents were forced to resort to using 'flying toilets' to dispose of their waste. The dominant historical perception of slums as dirty and diseased spaces is, therefore, largely shaped by socio-economic, technological and cultural inequalities that are perpetuated by wealthy groups.[41]

African cities are not alone in the substandard provision of public conveniences for the poor. Indian cities continue to face a severe shortage of toilet facilities: one study estimates that 15 million urban households across India lack access to basic sanitation and have to defecate outdoors. There is a major gender issue here because women have to wait until night-time to relieve themselves in adjacent fields or wastelands, which puts them at risk of personal danger. A 2011 study by WaterAid found that women living in the slums of Delhi and Bhopal reported incidents of girls under ten 'being raped while on their way to use a public toilet'. More than

20 per cent of women interviewed reported walking a kilo-metre or more to defecate. Many women avoid eating or drinking in the daytime to avoid having to go to the open fields, which results in indigestion, stomach aches, loss of appetite and related health risks.[42]

As these examples illustrate, the gendered structuring of space within the context of the slum has long attracted his-torical interest. Mayne notes that late Victorian slum tourists used 'woman' as one of the main protagonists in their slum narratives. Press coverage of the police courts often con-trasted the 'slovenly slumwoman' with the middle-class 'good homemaker'; the former was an allegory for the slum itself and the poor life choices of its inhabitants, while the latter visualized the virtues of a bourgeois lifestyle.[43] More recently, women activists have been shown to play a positive role in agitating for the provision of improved housing and infra-structural services in slums like Brazil's *favelas*. Fischer has shown how the growth of Rio de Janeiro's self-built *favelas* between the 1930s and 1960s was the result of a confluence of factors, including extensive rural-to-urban migration, a casualized and low-paid labour force (with a sizeable propor-tion of working women employed as cooks, maids and nannies in middle-class homes), a lack of affordable housing and a growing agitation for citizen rights, especially from women. This contributed to the growth of a huge illegal city on the hillsides of the capital, of upwards of 1 million resi-dents, who faced the constant threat of eviction and demoli-tion of their homes. Whenever the bulldozers arrived to demolish the *favelas*, they usually faced women and children as the first line of defence. Women frequently complained when their families were rehoused in new housing projects during the 1960s, on the grounds that they were too small, distant and expensive, and 'they resented the dismantling of their family and community networks'.[44]

Women also faced difficulties in maintaining their homes in the *favelas*, having to contend with patchy public services at best. Piracy of electricity and other services was widely tolerated. Women were obliged to participate in unofficial, often illegal, networks of power and influence with local criminal gangs to buy access to services. A language of rights subsequently developed in the *favelas'* popular political culture, which drew upon gendered stereotypes of women lugging heavy water jugs up the *morros'* steep and muddy pathways to argue in favour of improvements. As Fischer notes, 'the back-breaking task was blamed for everything from washerwomen's inability to work to children's lack of schooling to a litany of health problems'.[45]

We have seen how the formation and negotiation of different social identities have been inextricably rooted in spatial changes within towns and cities across the world. Socio-spatial segregation and residential exclusion are embedded in the process of urbanization itself, and have taken both material and linguistic form. Segregation was generated and entrenched through people's access to an unequal property market, as well as elite perceptions of how urban populations lived their lives and how these subsequently fed into municipal policies. Slums and suburbs, however defined, are a product of social, economic, political and cultural inequalities and resource dependencies, and are inextricably linked to each other, as comparative research amply demonstrates.

While class, status and income continue to attract the lion's share of attention from urban historians, there is a growing literature that explores alternative readings of spatial segregation, notably from the perspective of gender, sexuality, race and ethnicity. This has arguably had a more significant bearing on research into other parts of the city that have not featured heavily in this chapter – notably the street and the city centre – and we will inevitably return to the theme of socio-spatial segregation in later chapters. We are left, however, with a pressing need to further explore the ways that the residents of these communities defined and articulated their own individual identities, rather than continuing to focus on elite representations. We need to know more about how individuals shaped their own identities and rooted these in space, alongside the more conventional approach of researching how identity is shaped by external forces and actors. There is a particular need to further explore the ways that alternative groups – working women, gays and lesbians, the young and elderly, for example – acted upon their residential spaces in the articulation of their own identities or had their identities shaped by the ideological and material constraints of their surrounding environments.

3

Governing Cities

> To foresee the rational extension of a human agglomeration;
> provide it with open space and sufficient air; provide for its
> upkeep, protect it against epidemics of all sorts, provide trans-
> portation, provide clean water, remove waste, improve housing,
> choose the best form of lighting, inspect food and milk...protect
> infants, modernize the school...provide hygiene, social services,
> fight against infectious diseases, improve our hospitals, shelters,
> nurseries.[1]

This quotation, from Edouard Herriot, Lyon's long-serving
mayor (1905–57), illustrates the importance of local government for managing urban environments and improving the
lives of city residents around the turn of the twentieth century.
It reveals the diverse range of services that municipal councils
were responsible for providing by 1900. These ranged from
public safety services like policing, fire-fighting, and street
lighting, to public health services such as street cleaning,
hygiene and medical care; they also encompassed a range of
educational services. They were the culmination of a long,
incremental history of public service provision, which
involved municipal and extra-municipal actors and dated
from the seventeenth century and earlier in some cases. Even
then, William Cohen, in his excellent comparative study of
urban government in provincial French cities, depicts considerable variety and diversity in the provision of local services

over time and from place to place. Herriot's comments high-light the significance of municipal autonomy in organizing and delivering public services locally, thereby challenging our assumptions about the centralized nature of post-revolution-ary French political life.

Herriot's comments further reveal the importance of people – mayors, elected councillors, city managers and offi-cials, workers and so on – to the expansion and consolidation of urban government. A combination of inspection, improve-ment and regulation, and a growing municipal budget, meant that industrializing cities established large bureaucracies of professional, qualified officials with specialized expertise, who were responsible for ensuring that services were pro-vided efficiently and economically. By the late twentieth century, the management of a city's affairs had become a mammoth task with many Western cities starting to hire chief executive officers to oversee the business. But the mayor – or the provost in Scotland, or burgomaster in Germany – con-tinued to symbolize a city's historical and contemporary status; some, especially those of the major metropolises in the world, have enjoyed a degree of power 'closer to that of a head of state'. In 1977, when Ed Koch became New York's mayor, he controlled an annual budget of more than \$10 billion (at the time the eleventh-largest governmental budget in the world), was responsible for a police force 22,000 strong, and had direct or indirect responsibility for hospitals, welfare and schools, fire, sanitation, transportation, public housing, and more than 25,000 acres of parks and playgrounds.[2]

The literature on urban government and governance has conventionally taken the urban elite to be the core focus of its study, and situated it within both the institutional history of local government and the wider social, economic and cultural context of the city and nation. Empirical research has revealed how the practice of urban government has encapsulated groups and activities that extend far wider than local governments per se: voluntary associations, land trust-ees, religious orders and trade unions have also played key roles in governing the urban environment. So too have mate-rial technologies and practices, and this chapter will intro-duce the three overlapping historiographical waves of urban government, arguing that the emerging literature on governmentality (the art and materiality of government) needs to better integrate the methods and approach utilized by the earlier generation of scholarship.

Urban Government and the Social Composition of Elites

> I do not think that enough really able people are interested to-day in taking part in local government. I do not think that enough people from business, from industry, from agriculture and the professions are going into it...Most people engaged or interested in local government agree...that the calibre of local government is not equal all round to its responsibilities.[3]

These criticisms from Evelyn Sharp, the Permanent Secretary of the British Government's Ministry of Housing and Local Government, to delegates at the Annual Conference of the Association of Municipal Corporations in 1960, attracted the attentions of a diverse array of scholars, including political scientists, sociologists and urban historians, interested in the changing ways in which towns and cities have been governed across time. A key topic of discussion at the international round-table conference of the Urban History Group in 1966 concerned the social composition of urban local government. One of the participants at this conference was E. P. Hennock, who spoke about the composition of the Leeds and Birmingham town councils during the nineteenth century.

In his monumental study, *Fit and Proper Persons: Ideal and Reality in Urban Government*, Hennock expanded his remit beyond its comparative dimension in order to address these contemporaneous concerns about the declining standards in local government. He cited the rise since 1914 of the paid official – with his loyalty to his profession rather than his employer, and his increasingly specialized vocabulary – as playing a significant role in explaining contemporaneous concerns about the alleged decline in the quality of elected local representatives. In addition to this, growing centralization of public services, involving the imposition of national minimum standards of service delivery, inspection and certification, as well as increasingly large grants funded from general taxation, were recognized as tipping the balance of financial and legal power in favour of central government, at the direct expense of local autonomy.[4]

Hennock's book remains a crucial read for urban historians because he shows how many of Sharp's concerns were not new to the post-war world of local government. Recognizing the difficulty of quantifying 'quality' or 'ability', Hennock explored the socio-economic composition of the elites who comprised the elected municipal corporations established in Leeds and Birmingham following their adoption of the 1835 Municipal Corporations Act, in 1835 and 1838 respectively. This Act – alongside the 1833 Burgh Police (Scotland) Act – heralded a transformation in the structure and organization of urban government across Britain, introduced probity and accountability into municipal life, and made public office an attractive prospect for local elites. Even those historians who question the extent to which the Acts revolutionized municipal government – citing longer-term and piecemeal improvements to public office and local services during the eighteenth and early nineteenth centuries – recognize that towns and cities were better governed in 1914 than they were in 1835 and, further, that they were generally governed by a better calibre of councillor.[5]

Innovative and systematic in his methodology, Hennock drew upon an impressive range of published and unpublished sources – newspapers, census records, trade directories, annual reports of clubs and societies, business and religious records, municipal proceedings and branch records for political parties – to build a compositional profile of elected representatives on the two councils in order to determine whether municipal corporations between 1835 and 1914 drew upon the services of those most prominent in the economic and social life of their town. Hennock therefore defined an elite group through occupational data, identifying their interests and influence through their ownership of businesses, the size of their workforce, and the capital employed. His justification for focusing predominantly on councillors' business backgrounds stemmed from the view that, certainly before 1914, English town councils were reliant on being administered by those with 'a marked flair for business', particularly given that 'it was essential in order to achieve anything to be able to think adventurously about finance'. His data was derived from twelve samples: eight were taken at decennial intervals in the January following the census year; the remaining four were taken at twenty-year intervals in mid-decade, i.e., January 1836, 1856, 1876 and 1896. Unsurprisingly, his 'Note on Methods', contained in the appendix to the book, has proven to be well-thumbed ever since by doctoral students (including myself) who have been strongly influenced by his sampling technique, linkage of data and comparative approach.[6]

As might be expected from such a systematic study, Hennock found significant variety of interests in both towns across the period. Both underwent fluctuating fortunes in the quality of their elected representatives at this time; Sharp's criticisms were as applicable to different towns at different dates during the nineteenth century as they were in 1960, but the obverse is equally true. Birmingham Town Council suffered from a mediocre membership until 1862, after which it benefited from the influence of large business-men and professionals like the screw manufacturers Joseph Chamberlain and J. S. Nettlefold and the auctioneer Samuel Edwards, all of whom were actively engaged in municipal affairs. During the ensuing thirty-year period, Birmingham – under the aegis of the 'Civic Gospel' – became renowned for its innovation in the provision of public services, famously buying up the town's gas, water, electricity and tramway interests in order to run them as municipal enterprises, but also pioneering the professionalization of fire protection and police administration.

Leeds, on the other hand, enjoyed a period of activity from 1835 that culminated with the passage of its local Improvement Act in 1842, which promised significant public health improvements for the town. Hennock put this down to the shift in power from an oligarchic corporation run by anti-reformist Anglicans to a new municipal corporation under the control of a reformist dissenting elite of merchants, manufacturers and professionals. Yet these improvements were subsequently delayed by an influx of economy interests in the ensuing decade, involving councillors who were determined to defend rate-payers' interests against what were regarded

as expensive interventions. In fact, Leeds suffered from periodic bursts of activity followed by inertia until the 1890s
when a bi-partisan consensus emerged between Liberals and
Conservatives to pursue social reforms, which continued for
the next twenty years. It was, agued Hennock, no coincidence
that this newfound engagement correlated with a rise in the
number of businessmen and professionals and drew inspiration from the earlier example set by Birmingham.

There are problems with Hennock's study, not least his
assertion that there existed a link between the size of a
business and the quality of public service. The assumption
that small businessmen like shopkeepers and publicans –
the 'shopocracy' – were more interested in reducing local
rates than in improving public services has since been challenged. The petite bourgeoisie were not as parsimonious
as Hennock suggests; indeed, they invariably played key
roles in transforming city centres throughout the nineteenth
century, as research by Geoffrey Crossick, Heinz-Gerhard
Haupt, Barry Doyle and others has shown, and were also
significant rate-payers as owners of residential rental property as well as commercial businesses. Shopkeepers also
proved to be popular with the electorate well into the
twentieth century, outlasting the manufacturer in the age
of mass suffrage.[7]

Hennock's conclusions were never intended as a generalization across the country or period as a whole; subsequently,
various additional towns and cities have received similar
attention. The majority have sensibly utilized detailed compositional analysis, with methodological or temporal revi-
sions that have added to the complexity and variety of
available models. John Garrard opened his comparative
study up to three medium-sized industrial towns (Bolton,
Oldham and Rochdale) and considered the importance of
non-decision-making as an equal measure of power to
policymaking; Richard Trainor widened his focus on to the
metropolitan region, exploring the relationships forged by
urban elites across the Black Country in the West Midlands;
while Barry Doyle extended the chronological focus of the
literature into the interwar period with his study of Norwich,
revealing more continuities in membership than Hennock
noted for his cases.[8]

Others have scrutinized the century leading up to the passage of the Municipal Corporations Act. Louise Miskell, for example, has examined how industrialists migrated to eighteenth- and early nineteenth-century Swansea, where, excluded from municipal office by a self-elected elite, they built strong familial and social links amongst themselves in order to oust their competitors once the Act was passed. Furthermore, Penelope Corfield and Rosemary Sweet have both illustrated how notions of public service and communal responsibility shaped the work of the pre-reformed councils and the growing number of improvement and police commissioners created in the eighteenth century. The quality of service might have varied from town to town, but the problems that faced industrializing towns were so unprecedented and technical knowledge so constantly evolving that it became difficult to find suitable solutions.[9]

More recently still, the focus has shifted on to the variations of administrative expertise within individual councils: my own research has revealed how certain committees, like the watch committee (which was responsible for administering policing and other public safety services in English municipal corporations), were more prestigious than others and, as a result, attracted the services of a higher calibre of elite. Hennock alluded to this being the case in late Victorian Birmingham, but he did not pay attention to the working relationships formed between elected representatives and their chief officials, which considerably influenced decision-making from *c*.1870. James Moore and Richard Rodger similarly recognize the considerable prestige attached to certain committees, which they describe as 'semi-autonomous fiefdoms ruled by their chairman'. It obviously meant more to chair the watch, gas or water committees – with their large budgets and departmental staff – than it did to chair parks, nuisances or general purposes; in the twentieth century the housing portfolio became the jewel in the municipal crown.[10]

Studies of twentieth-century urban government further reveal the difficulties in generalization. Sharp's insinuation that local government was in general decline is difficult to support given the continued variations in quality and practice across the country. Nick Hayes and Barry Doyle, for instance, have shown how, in provincial English cities like Nottingham and Norwich, municipalities continued to attract good-quality councillors well into the 1930s and 1940s, loyal to their city over their party political obligations. Examples abound of consensual cross-party politics, including the distribution of key committee posts like chair, to a far greater extent than the alleged 'golden age' of Victorian local government (though Hennock never argued that there ever existed such an age).[11]

Similar cases have been explored in relation to twentieth-century European municipalities during an age of mass politics. In interwar Amsterdam, for instance, new political leaders – like the social democratic mayor Willem de Vlugt (1921–41), a local self-made artisan, and the socialist Floor Wibaut (1914–31), an outsider from Zeeland who amassed a fortune from the wood industry – were able to access the corridors of municipal power hitherto monopolized by the traditional conservative-liberal elite. With new parties and social backgrounds came an impetus to develop social welfare policies locally, especially in the fields of housing and planning. Conterminously, a new group of active experts emerged, comprised of paid municipal directors who, through their day-to-day running of municipal offices and membership of associational bodies, acquired for themselves a heightened status within municipal government. Although quarrels broke out between these officials and their elected representatives over the former's efforts to define themselves as a new urban elite, their ambitions were reined in by equally powerful elected elites who were no less capable of running a thriving metropolis or asserting their political authority than Amsterdam's old elite.[12]

The dual pressures of administrative reform and traditional socio-cultural ties also came to bear upon the governing apparatus of Meiji Japan cities, Ottoman cities like the capital Istanbul, Tunis and Tripoli, and China's republican-era cities. Seki Hajime, mayor of Osaka from 1923 until 1935, was an exemplar of a mindset that was rooted in national culture as well as modernizing Western-inspired administrative systems. He led the Osaka municipality during a crucial period in its modern history, and undertook important urban and social reforms, rather than relying on the national government. In so doing, Seki drew on a network of neighbourhood associations, voluntary bodies and new managerial classes, combined with the lessons from his own studies and travels across Western Europe, to devise solutions to the industrial city's problems.[13]

The loosening of long-standing imperial bonds over local communities and everyday life created a power vacuum which new elite groups were subsequently able to fill. Christian Henriot has traced the relationship between the decline in imperial authority and the rise of local merchant elites in modernizing Shanghai's municipality for a decade from 1927, identifying several notable families who used traditional ties of family, kin and friendship to govern their city. These families used their connections across Shanghai's civil society to shore up their power base, as well as to coordinate local service provision. They thus assumed responsibility for managing the harbour, maintaining roads and bridges, lighting and cleaning the streets, and administering policing and poor-relief services. Using similar methods to Hennock, Henriot reveals the importance of *guanxi* (interpersonal ties) to the running of the Shanghai municipality during this period: mayors preferred to hire senior officials from their native province, who, in turn, looked to trusted families and friends to staff their bureaucracies. Turnover amongst municipal staffs was relatively high, being pegged to the rotation of the mayoralty and other senior office-holdings, which stunted any continuity in municipal policymaking across the period. Henriot is left to describe the situation as local government by civil servants (*defang guanzhi*), rather than local self-government (*defang zizhi*).[14]

These cases reveal the interplay between elite groups and administrative structures in shaping the expansion of urban government. Detailed compositional studies based on municipal proceedings help peel back the layers of urban government and reveal the personal, professional and political connections between elites across a plethora of institutional and quasi-institutional bodies. They are useful exercises in reconstructing the composition of urban elites across the entirety of urban civil society. Paraphrasing the anthropologist Clifford Geertz, they enable urban historians to provide 'thick descriptions' of the beliefs and prejudices of individual city politicians, officials and administrators; it is only by tracing the individual and collective life histories of the actors that a fuller picture of governing practices can be produced.[15] Sharp's comments about the alleged decline of local government in England, then, fail to consider the broader 'world of local government', as it is known in political science, in which non-governmental bodies such as charities or voluntary societies created an overlapping, interdependent sphere within which elites prospered long after the shift in the balance between the centre and its local agencies. She defines local government in its narrowest sense: as a formal agent of central government, thereby overlooking a wide range of bodies, people and resources. This signals a changed approach in the field, to situating urban government within the broader parameters of urban *governance*, to seeing the town council as one of a number of institutions that comprised civil society.

From Government to Governance

Urban governance is, as the name indicates, broader than urban government per se. R. J. Morris helpfully defines governance as being concerned with 'the ordering of order, and...the organization and legitimization of authority', which inevitably opens up the field of inquiry on to a wider spectrum of social actors and interests.[16] For example, Ralf Roth cites Johann Christian Senckenberg, a philanthropist in early modern Frankfurt, as a member of the elite class who never held an official political position in the city. Instead, he set up a foundation in 1763 to establish a hospital for the city, as well as a centre for the study of natural sciences. As a member of the German burgher class – the wealthy, educated, urban middle-class – Senckenberg illustrates how nonpolitical elites could still exert a 'tremendous influence on urban political, economic and cultural developments'. Roth subsequently identifies three elite groups across fourteen German cities in the eighteenth and nineteenth centuries: political leaders (*politische Führungsshicht*) drawn from municipal institutions; economic leaders and taxpayers (*wirtschaftliche Oberschicht*); and opinion leaders (*kulturelle Elite*) elevated to elite status through their participation in philanthropic, religious and sundry bodies. Notwithstanding this picture of a heterogeneous urban elite, comprised of different religious backgrounds and political persuasions, and working across multiple institutions (philanthropic foundations, guilds, boards of trade, churches, clubs and societies, as well as local government), Roth concedes that its membership had a shared concern for maintaining order and public safety in their growing communities.[17]

It was this interest in public safety and the protection of private property that encouraged the urban propertied classes to develop a keen interest in establishing voluntary societies to regulate social spaces and human activities, particularly during the period 1780–1850. Although these societies were bodies separate from urban local government, they invariably shared many interests and concerns through their overlapping membership. In Frankfurt during the 1830s alone, Roth identifies more than 3,000 burghers – or over 50 per cent of the city's burghers – participating in over thirty different societies. In his pioneering study of the Leeds middle class, R. J. Morris charts a similarly unprecedented growth in the number and variety of voluntary societies, with predominantly middle-class memberships united by a shared concern about the growing complexity and anonymity of the industrial town. They included, amongst others, mechanics institutes, literary and philosophical societies, circulating libraries, friendly and temperance societies, medical charities, trade unions, brass bands and gardening clubs, while their subscription lists boasted the names of the same sort of 'fit and proper persons' studied by Hennock. At their heart was a shared commitment to establishing and maintaining a healthy civil society governed by the rule of law, private property, an active commerce, and the development of arts and manufactures. The assumption was that societies such as these were better placed than local government to promote social cohesion and interclass cooperation since they tended to operate through more informal and everyday channels than the municipal authorities. As Morris comments, civil society 'needed to operate in a way which mediated between people and government, between the prescriptive agency of the state and the private sphere of the individual'.[18]

This understanding of civil society as a combination of institutional and extra-institutional forms and discourses,

autonomous from, but linked to, the state, was not limited
to the Western world, or indeed the modern period. During
the medieval period, the ascendancy of Islamic cities across
the Middle East may have been achieved without the sort of
civic autonomy and burghal leadership that Max Weber identified for the European city. However, the spread and consolidation of an Islamic urban power-base was aided by
informal power structures and networks within and between
cities, such as neighbourhood districts (*mahalles*), guilds and
waqfs. The *waqf* (or *vakif*, in Turkish, which is usually translated as 'pious foundation' or 'religious endowment') played
a crucial role in urban governance, providing much of the
infrastructure for urban commerce and welfare organization
from the earliest times in Islamic history. Variously responsible for the provision of urban services and social meeting
places, the stimulation of commercial activities, the provision
of poor relief and the regulation of the land rental market,
they were, Ebru Boyar writes, 'a central pillar of the urban
fabric'. Moreover, they were never merely the preserve of the
sultans or senior officials, but also incorporated men of
modest wealth like the locksmith Elhaç Hüseyin, who, in
1783, had a large fountain erected in the market of Balıkesir,
in the Marmara region of Turkey, the water from which
subsequently supplied smaller fountains in six *mahalles* of
the city. He also set up a *waqf* from the income of two
shops and a mill to provide for the maintenance of these
fountains.[19]

In *Urban Governance: Britain and Beyond since 1750*,
Morris describes governance as being concerned with the
procedures through which a political system operates, as well
as the institutions that constitute it, stating that it refers to
'the patterns and processes which create and organize authority, provide access to resources, provide for the delivery of
services, and generate and deliver policy'.[20] Voluntary societies have, therefore, played a crucial role in governing all types
of cities and, as a result, the structure and membership of
such bodies have historically mirrored the power structure
of an urban community at large. Morris cites the example
of the Edinburgh Society for the Suppression of Beggars,
founded in 1813 to eliminate the practice of street begging
in the city. Its membership overlapped strongly with the city's

political, legal and religious establishments, and its activities were supported by a number of interested merchants and shopkeepers, as well as a committee of ladies. Its work involved collecting and publishing information on the problem, through which it sought to influence council policy. It also established and maintained links with other organizations through a commitment to transparency: its activities were conducted in the public sphere through annual general meetings, reports and the publication of subscription lists in local newspapers. These information flows were the means by which civil society was legitimated and strengthened, providing a clear link between the institutional and extra-institutional governing bodies in the city; this has been reinforced by studies of other Western European cities, especially in the Low Countries by Boudien de Vries, Jan Hein Furnée and others.[21]

Longitudinal studies have revealed the importance of interactions between formal and informal networks, as well as circulations of knowledge to maintaining social cohesion in fast-growing cities. In his study of land, property and trust in Edinburgh, Richard Rodger shows how the formal institutional relationships forged between local government, the law and local firms were linked into a wider web of connections, involving multiple subscriber societies. Together, these alliances between local business and political elites were the product of a pluralist conception of power that was dependent upon trust-based relationships. House building, slum clearance and property development in nineteenth-century Edinburgh were tied together by the legal and institutional framework of property rights, combined with the management and redistribution of property income through trustees over a long period of time, many of which used the funds to provide public services or to regulate street improvements. For example, George Heriot's trustees used the income derived from land purchases to establish, initially, in 1659, a 'hospital' (a charitable school for fatherless children) and, from the 1830s, free foundation schools to educate poor children in all areas of the city. When the schools were absorbed into the municipal school system in 1886, the historic connections between voluntarism and municipal enterprise were formally enshrined.[22]

The literature thus reveals how important openness and transparency were to explaining the rise of modern urban governance. As Alan DiGaetano explains in his comparative study of the municipal regimes in eighteenth- and nineteenth-century Boston, Massachusetts, and Bristol, England, three basic characteristics define the rise of modern (post-1700) urban governance: first, a clear division between the public and private domains; second, direct provision of services by agencies of urban government; and, third, the formation of institutional mechanisms for democratic accountability. While there is less agreement over the first point, there being a long tradition of overlap between the public and private provision of services (especially in public health and the utilities) across Asia, Europe and North America, the model provides a useful starting point for comparatively exploring the broad changes in the organization of urban governance in a transcontinental context. For DiGaetano, early modern towns failed to meet these three criteria adequately; instead, services were provided by a variety of public, quasi-public, private and voluntary bodies, with little attention paid to public scrutiny of their accounts. In eighteenth-century Boston, for example, the municipal government provided poor relief and educational services; policing and fire protection services were delivered by a combination of voluntary or quasi-public organization, including fire insurance companies; while sewers and bridges were maintained by private bodies.[23]

Meanwhile, before the passage of the Municipal Corporations Act, the Bristol Corporation was 'the only governing body of general competence, but it often eschewed any responsibility for the city's general welfare'.[24] The Corporation performed some licensing and inspecting responsibilities, but spent little on law and order or public health, whereas private bodies like the Dock Company and the Society of Merchant Venturers managed the docks and issued shipping licences. In addition, a growing number of quasi-public (that is, partly elected, but still largely self-appointing) bodies – the Select Vestry and Paving Commissioners, for example – performed functions including road repair, poor relief and street lighting. The same applied to other early industrial towns, where quasi-public bodies were engaged in protracted battles with private interests to take control over natural monopolies like water and the sewers.

Even after municipal reform, private and quasi-public bodies continued to provide important services. In Bristol and elsewhere, fire insurance companies continued to protect property from the threat of fire; private companies also provided water, gas and other energy services for large parts of the century. Representative local democracy and transparency was achieved in a piecemeal fashion: after 1835, all English and Welsh municipal corporations had to annually publish their accounts, but it invariably took rate-payers' interest groups to force them to fully open up their account books. Incorporation, institution building and transparency necessarily went hand-in-hand; only by the final quarter of the nineteenth century were the majority of municipal corporations in a sufficiently stable position to significantly expand their responsibilities into services hitherto left to the market to supply. The same conclusions are applicable to the North American experience of progressivism between the 1890s and 1920s, during which mayors and their cabinets started effectively scrutinizing municipal budgets in order to cut down on rate-payer complaints of corruption and cronyism. This opening up of government to public scrutiny, as well as its expansion into areas of social reform, in turn entailed a considerable increase in public revenues and expenditure, drawing upon a growing local fiscal base to fund expansion, which further reinforced the importance of financial prudence and openness.[25]

The research into urban governance, then, reveals a plurality of organizations that enjoyed access to the power structures of urban government, and offers scope for detailed longitudinal and comparative case studies. However, access remained restricted to a small property-owning elite, especially before the era of mass party politics that was ushered in during the final quarter of the nineteenth century and the first third of the twentieth. This reinforces Hennock's conclusions: that the urban elite was comprised of a cross-section of urban middle-class society and it was difficult for outsiders (the working class, and women, for instance) to access its official bodies until recent times. Thus, the compositional and governance perspectives remain top-down approaches, concerned as they are with the more or less formal structures and practices of power.

From Governance to Governmentality

A third, interrelated perspective on urban government has emerged since the 1990s, which is more interested in the operations of power from a postmodern perspective. In so doing, it is strongly influenced by the linguistic turn outlined in chapter 1 and the subsequent emerging interest in the materiality of cities. Urban governmentality, the art of government within complex urban environments, is heavily influenced by the writings of Michel Foucault, and inevitably demands closer attention to the materialities, technologies and practices of governing cities. This approach recognizes that power is a more dynamic and fluid force than hitherto recognized. This opens the field on to a wider range of social groups, while also enabling scrutiny of the ways in which power was practised locally through disciplinary technologies and social practices.

In his essay, 'On Governmentality', Foucault traces the emergence of the modern state (over a roughly 300-year period from the sixteenth century) as an apparatus of security responsible for the art of government at three levels of social relationships: first, the art of self-government; that is, of instilling in oneself the moral values of the particular age; second, the art of governing a family and running it economically; and, third, the art of being governed, by which people themselves accept being governed. This process of self-governance is achieved through the twin pillars of surveillance and objectification, followed by 'subjectification', in which the individual is transformed (and transforms him/her self) into a subject capable of systematic study and categorization (as sane/mad, heterosexual/homosexual, moral/deviant and so on). These new categories are subsequently established through a combination of legal, medical and governmental discourses and circulated through society via print, visual and oral cultures. Self-governance is thus achieved through the practices of power, which are localized in and around the body and its everyday social and cultural practices.[26]

Some urban historians have subsequently adopted a Foucauldian framework in their studies of nineteenth-century industrial cities. Patrick Joyce, in particular, has explored the ways in which the 'eye of power' was utilized in British cities to create the 'liberal individual' as a modern subject. In *The Rule of Freedom: Liberalism and the Modern City*, Joyce contends there was a need for power to be wielded in order to guarantee the freedom of the individual, as well as the individual's ability to govern his or her own actions and beliefs – and the modern city provided the means to do this. As the most highly urbanized society in the world, Britain provided the testing ground for the disciplinary practices of 'liberal governmentality'; that is, of finely balancing the freedom of the individual with the imperative to rule. Thus, the modern surveillance state emerged from the 1830s onwards and was committed to studying, objectifying and categorizing urban populations through statistical surveys, cartography, municipal inspections, the compilation of trade directories and the circulation of newspapers and other forms of print culture. Given the acute public health problems that blighted British cities at this time, it also involved viewing the city in pathological terms: as an organic entity that needed the building of hard engineering and the framing of anti-nuisance regulations in order to combat social and environmental problems. In material terms, this included the provision of waste-water systems or smoke abatement technologies to combat water and air pollution, the laying of tram and rail tracks in order to increase the circulation of people through the city streets, as well as the appointment of nuisance and sanitary inspectors, medical officers of health and other 'disinterested' experts. Joyce labels these practices as 'governing by numbers', through the use of specific tools utilized by the state and its agents to maximize control over society in the most legitimate (aka non-violent) way and, by extension, increase self-governance as well. Much of this activity was coordinated through urban government, using the new town halls built through the 1840s–80s and designed in a variety of historical architectural styles, which served as a symbol simultaneously of freedom, surveillance and, most of all, modernity (see chapter 5). The state was thus able to rule the individual and the family from afar because liberal democracy was a mode of rule by which the state gained legitimacy and credibility.[27]

Similarly, Chris Otter provides a postmodern reading of nineteenth-century urban governance, through the Foucauldian prism of governmentality, in *The Victorian Eye: A Political History of Light and Vision in Britain, 1800–1910*. In part a history of vision, light and the eye, Otter fuses an interest in the history of technology, the environment and political history to further illustrate how nineteenth-century liberalism was a mode of governmentality. He notes how 'liberal governmentality' had a conspicuously visual character in cities and, moreover, the lighting of particular urban spaces at different times of the day played a pivotal role in maintaining rule from afar. The use of modern lighting technologies – both in public with gas and, later, electric street lamps, as well as within the privacy of the home – cast light on to the darkness of urban spaces and regulated human behaviour through the 'eye of power'. The example of the 'Bulls' Eye' light used by police officers on their night beats illustrates how well-cast light can illuminate the social conditions of the bustling city, shedding light on even the darkest recesses at night. Indeed, the police force – both as an institution representing the law as well as a set of cultural practices – was significant in providing 'the eyes' for the liberal state and enacting 'liberal governmentality' locally. In combination with the local press, as studied by Andy Croll in his study of the Welsh mining town of Merthyr Tydfil, the social and cultural practices of Victorian urban populations were opened up to intense scrutiny through the practices of governmentality, which in turn sheds light on the (in)effectiveness of municipalities and their officials to control such spaces. For these historians, then, governmentality is as much about the materiality of urban spaces and the technologies that comprise them (ranging from heavy engineering to print culture) as it is about the people and institutions that formally govern them.[28]

As an innovative approach to the study of urban political power, the 'liberal governmentality' literature poses important questions about the agency of material technologies in adding a further layer of control to municipal power. In evolving out of the urban governance literature, it further reveals the multifarious patterns and practices through which authority is created, organized and diffused. Its biggest contribution – aside from the challenging theoretical questions it poses about the nature and practice of power – is in illustrating the mechanics of service technologies, dissecting the street lights, sewers and printing presses that were in operation. It therefore, as we shall see in chapter 4, shares much in common with established practices in urban environmental history, revealing urban history as a discipline at the intersection of numerous other disciplines, not least cultural history and the history of science and technology.

What it currently lacks, however, is a clearer connection with the literatures outlined earlier in this chapter, specifically the compositional studies prevalent in the history of urban government. In particular, with a few exceptions, the absence of comparative case studies or detailed urban biographies suggests that the 'liberal governmentality' process is more homogeneous and normative than its advocates would likely argue. However, given that street-lighting technologies were in place in seventeenth- and eighteenth-century towns, this illustrates how the practices of lighting, watching and policing owed their roots to local decision-making and investment, which, as historians like Malcolm Falkus have shown, inevitably took place on an incremental and haphazard basis.[29] A similarly localized process occurred in the provision of other governing technologies during the nineteenth and twentieth centuries, ranging from street fire hydrants to police call-boxes, traffic signals and Closed Circuit Television (CCTV). The explanations for these differences emanate from administrative practice and local decision-making: Birmingham Fire Brigade, for example, exercised full responsibility for hydrant provision from the 1880s and, recognizing the importance of having high-pressure water services spread across the city, invested more heavily in the technology; this was contrary to the practice adopted elsewhere, such as Leicester, where water departments maintained such responsibility, often more cheaply.[30]

We return, in conclusion, to the importance of conducting local and comparative case studies of urban governments – their members, committees and officials – and those other organizations that comprised urban civil society. Crucially, we also need to map out the resources at their disposal in designing, building and maintaining material technologies to aid them in their governance of local communities. This necessitates the sort of detailed archival research (drawing upon nominal record linkage methods) that Hennock pioneered. Comparisons can, of course, be drawn between towns and cities within a national framework, which reveal the importance of localized factors and access to specific resources in influencing the municipal reform process: studies cited here have done this. Further, as DiGaetano's study shows, comparisons across national borders reveal broad commonalities in the municipal experiences faced by cities with similar socio-economic and political structures. Care must be taken in selecting appropriate case studies, but where this has been done the results reveal the pluralist practice and diffusion of power at, across and in between the local level(s). Studies also echo a longer and wider history of civic and community involvement in the provision of services across Asia, the Middle East, Europe and North America.

Simultaneously, though, this emerging literature demands that the traditional compositional approach is taken outside the 'black box' of the municipality in order to embrace the technologies underpinning and connecting the different regimes and actors invested in governing modern cities.[31] This in turn demands expanding the database beyond the conventional elites of urban government (people like Herriot, Koch, Chamberlain and de Vlugt) to include the architects and engineers behind these material technologies, as well as the service providers, including their employees who maintained and ran them. Lamp-lighters, scavengers, fire-fighters, police officers and such like were involved in governing urban environments as much as those political elites who made the decisions to invest in new technologies or hire additional labour to manage them. So too were the members of the public, whose everyday lives were transformed by new technologies – including new planning practices, building materials, communications and safety regulations. Here one can take the cue from recent research into the history of governing and self-governing practices of everyday urban life and the cultural history of the emotions.[32] Only then can we truly appreciate the practice and flow of power relations from decision-making through to implementation, regulation, conformity and resistance.

4
Cities and the Environment

Understanding cities and the city-building process is essential for understanding environmental change. This is unsurprising given how the unfettered growth of cities over the last few hundred years has had a detrimental effect on ecosystems across the world. Although a start has been made in the Western world at tackling the long-term effects of environmental deterioration brought on by industrialization, the environmental conditions of rapid urbanization in the developing world remain bleak, impacting greatly on pollution and land use, while their ecological footprints – that is to say, the space that a city needs to support its activities and absorb its wastes – have grown exponentially. While this has also stimulated an international interest in global environmental problems – as witnessed by the United Nations' Earth Summit in Rio de Janeiro in 1992 and its successor conference on sustainable development, Rio+20, in 2012 – the recalcitrance of nation-states to seriously tackle climate change continues to bedevil real reform. The decision to host these flagship conferences in a city that suffers from severely poor air quality, water pollution, a high cost of living and an acute (and historical) problem with shanty housing has not been lost on some commentators. Protests on the streets of Rio and other Brazilian cities during 2013–14 further highlight the social and environmental inequalities that are rife in this fast-growing country; the eyes of the world are fixed on Rio as it prepares to host the Olympic Games in 2016, two years after Brazil hosted the FIFA World Cup.[1]

Given their shared interest in cities, urban and environmental history make natural bedfellows. One of the leading protagonists of taking an urban approach to environmental history, Joel Tarr, has admitted that 'I have always thought of myself as an urban rather than [an] environmental historian.'[2] Urban environmental history has, since the 1990s, emerged as a vibrant subfield of environmental history, sharing urban history's predilection for the comparative case-study-led approach. As Martin Melosi, another leading specialist, notes, this subfield's growth is itself a challenge to the belief amongst some environmental historians that there exist two environments: 'a natural world that tends to exclude humans, and an artificial world – a built environment – that is solely the product of human action'.[3]

The rise of urban environmental history is itself evidence that environmental history is no longer a new field of study; it also reflects the consensus that cities have a vital role to play in tackling issues related to climate change, sustainability and energy efficiency. With its origins in the environmental movement of the 1960s and 1970s, some of the early path-breaking work has been subject to criticism from urban historians. However, environmental history continues to offer a radical and politicized alternative to mainstream historical fields. Some rightly argue that mainstream historians could learn much from the alternative source base and methodological approaches practised by environmental historians. In particular, the focus on material culture (including dirt and other forms of matter as well as hard engineering and socio-technologies more generally) and human interactions with the environment has put urban environmental historians in the vanguard of the more recent epistemological shift away from the cultural to the material; that is, 'from questions of representation to matters of process, practice and effect' and a renewed focus on the cultural geographies of cities.[4] Melosi, for instance, contends that 'environmental history has done much more than most fields to be bold, inclusive, and creative in pushing forward the value of the field of history itself...it established no clear boundaries, was accepting of new ideas, and was not afraid to look beyond disciplinary walls for

those ideas.' Cities have been singled out as 'the most important outlet' for giving environmental history an edge in order
to confront the big problems of the day.[5] It is this inclusivity,
creativity, edginess and interdisciplinarity that link the two
fields. Urban historians are at home with environmental
approaches to studying the past because, as we shall see, they
share common methods, use a similar variety of traditional
and non-traditional sources, and are not constrained by a
disciplinary straitjacket in seeking answers to historical questions about the creation, use and management of the urban
environment.

Varieties of Environmental History

Donald Worster was the first environmental historian to seek
to outline the field of inquiry, boldly proposing that 'environmental history is about the role and place of nature in human
life. By common understanding we mean by "nature" the
nonhuman world, the world we have not in any primary
sense created.'[6] Noting that the field was 'born out of a strong
moral concern' with the worsening environmental condition
of the planet, Worster rejected the assumption that human
history was separate from nature and 'that the ecological
consequences of our past deeds can be ignored'.[7] There are
two major forces that have realigned man's relationship with
nature since early modern times: demographic changes, but
especially population increase and rising out-migration, and
political economy, notably the rise of the global capitalist
economy and industrialization, which was built on the intensive use of fossil fuels, first coal, later gas and oil. It was,
according to ecologists and geologists, during this new geological epoch, the anthropocene, that the human species
emerged as a geological force in its own right, capable of
acting as 'a force of nature in the geological sense'.[8]

In studying the agency of nature and matter in human life,
environmental historians are forced to interrogate a wider
array of primary sources other than conventional documents:
these include scientific data derived from diatom analysis
or dendrochronology, for example, geological and archaeo-
logical evidence, and the landscape around us. Worster's

definition, in a nutshell, explains why environmental history has been at the margins of mainstream historical enquiry since its origins: most historians prefer to work with printed documents and shy away from scientific data. Very few – outside of urban or local history – are comfortable working with the landscape around them.

Worster subsequently outlined a three-point research agenda for doing environmental history. It involves, first, understanding nature itself; that is, the structure and dynamics of natural ecosystems in their own right. Second, the socio-economic realm of nature requires scrutiny, in exploring the material and technological impact on nature, subjecting it to man's control through agriculture, industrialization and urbanization. Third, we then have the study of cognitive landscapes, of tracing the changing ideological and cultural beliefs about nature.[9] While this appears to be applicable to the urban environment, Worster explicitly excludes it from his agenda. In a 1988 essay, he defines the 'social environment' as 'the scene of humans interacting only with each other in the absence of nature'. For Worster, this included the built environment, which he dismissed as 'wholly expressive of culture', separate from nature, and subsequently excluded from his agenda. The environmental historian should eschew solely cultural approaches to historical change in favour of natural forces and energies that are autonomous to human actions.[10]

There is an obvious contradiction here between calling for an integrative approach to the study of environmental history and rejecting scrutiny of the role played by cities and other 'social environments' in changing the natural environment, or indeed of the influence of nature in shaping the built environment itself (how Worster accounts for the presence of mammals, birds, plant life or soil in cities goes unaddressed). The celebrated environmental historian William Cronon criticizes Worster's failure to capture 'the full diversity of environmental history as a field dedicated to discovering "the role and place of nature in human life"'.[11] Moreover, Melosi convincingly challenges the declensionist narrative in environmental history – that humans have actively exploited and despoiled the inactive environment – and highlights some of the ways in which nature has acted upon humans and shaped the built environment. He quotes the well-known urban activist Jane Jacobs to illustrate this: 'Human beings are, of course, a part of nature, as much so as grizzly bears or bees or whales or sorghum cane. The cities of human beings are as natural, being a product of one form of nature as are the colonies of prairie dogs or the beds of oysters.' Given this fact, it is worthwhile plotting an alternative narrative to the declensionist one, which plays up the presence of nature in cities and breaks down the misguided belief that the natural and built environments are unconnected. Indeed, the growing belief amongst scientists and policymakers that cities can help solve environmental problems through sustainable planning and more efficient energy use points to the ever-increasing importance of historicizing cities' relationships to the natural environment, in order to overcome this nature/society dualism.[12]

The most influential research agenda for integrating built and natural environments has been Christine Meisner Rosen and Joel Tarr's introduction to a special issue of the *Journal of Urban History* in 1994. They offer a constructive alternative to Worster's agro-ecological model, and persuasively argue that the natural and built environments should be studied together:

> ...the natural and built environments evolved in dialectical inter-dependence and tension. The former influenced the technologies, materials, and locations chosen to construct the latter, with the built environment, in turn, modifying the land, climate, water cycles, and biological ecosystems of nature in an ongoing process of mutual interaction. Rather than peripheral to the concerns of environmental historians, the built environment is central.[13]

First, they outline the impact of cities on the natural environment, in placing demands on the countryside for food, water, fuel, building materials and waste disposal. Here they draw inspiration from Cronon's study of Chicago, whose ecological footprint is traced across the Midwest of North America based on its growth as a centre for meat-packing and grain and lumber distribution. Entire regions converted to livestock farming to serve Chicago's meat industry; it was the demand by city dwellers for food that drove the changes to capitalist agriculture that Worster refers to elsewhere.

Chicago's boosters even appropriated mythical nature – the phoenix bird – for its own metaphorical rebirth following its 'great fire' of 8–9 October 1871, which burned an area of 4 square miles and razed over 18,000 buildings, including the downtown business district and thousands of homes and small businesses. Roughly a third of the city's approximate 300,000 residents were left homeless, while almost 300 died. Neither did nature escape the destruction: trees, shrubs and plants were destroyed along the 120 miles of sidewalk burned. For all the destruction, the city was quickly rebuilt, and is often likened to the great phoenix rising from the ashes. Despite the widespread destruction, much of its commercial infrastructure on the south and west sides – its grain elevators, packing plants, lumber yards, and wharfs – remained largely intact, which fuelled the city's rapid reconstruction.[14]

Tarr and Rosen's second stage is to illustrate how nature has impacted upon cities, both in bestowing natural resources on residents and equally in playing a dramatic, destructive role in threatening urban order and human lives. To refer to Chicago again, its 'great fire' broke out following months of drought; only two and a half inches of rain had fallen during the summer and autumn, which, coupled with a driving south-westerly gale-force wind, inevitably meant that the city's wooden-lined buildings and sidewalks were easily ignited. The city had already suffered many fires since the summer, including a large mill blaze, attended by 185 firefighters, the previous night. Carl Smith and Karen Sawislak's studies of the social and cultural impacts of the fire further illustrate how contemporary debates about the city's water supply were shrouded in controversy surrounding its inevitable burning (the fire eventually burnt itself out, aided by a fresh fall of rain), while the ravages caused by the fire meant that the city's boosters could rebuild the city, simultaneously phasing out its obsolescent wooden housing stock, and get to grips with natural forces *within* the city. Chicago was a booster city of the Industrial Revolution, hence the fire represented its chaotic growth and the volatility associated with this.[15]

Third, Rosen and Tarr posit that we need to study urban society's response to environmental change, through the organization of government and the market, and the construction and management of technological systems. Sawislak illustrates how Chicago's great fire acted as a social force in integrating Chicagoans to provide relief and charity to the thousands of victims, while Rosen herself has shown how the creation of fire-proof zones in Chicago's meat-packing, lumber and manufacturing districts in the fire's aftermath gave the city's planners greater control over the destructive forces of nature. Political tensions between the city's administrators culminated in major changes to the city's administration, the safety rules governing private firms and the city's physical and spatial land-use patterns.[16]

Fourth, Rosen and Tarr reiterate the centrality of cities – through the long geographical and cultural reach of their buildings, transport infrastructure and power systems – to the earth's environmental history. On the same day as Chicago's conflagration, a forest fire broke out to the north of Peshtigo, in Wisconsin, killing over a thousand people, a far greater death toll than Chicago.[17] Yet it is Chicago that is remembered and commemorated – by historians, museum curators, documentary film-makers, social media and the general public – because of its wider social, economic and political impact, as well as the powerful cultural hold that it exerts over social memory.[18] The Chicago fire *is* integral to Chicagoans' modern environmental history, but its shadow clearly extends further still because of its historic attraction to so many people across the world.

Ploughing the Urban Field

Since both Rosen and Tarr's specialisms are in the history of urban technologies, their influence is most clearly discernible in the voluminous histories of urban technical infrastructures and their impacts on ecological systems. The construction and regulation of urban infrastructures has proven to be one of the most fertile grounds for urban and urban-environmental historians to furrow, and pre-dates the turn towards material history in the late 1990s. The best of this research situates itself in comparative case studies, seeking connections between cities, usually within a single nation.[19] More recent edited collections of case-study histories provide another way to explore the comparative dimension (the European literature is excellent at providing such compendiums), while a few studies ambitiously attempt cross-national comparisons themselves.[20]

One such cross-national comparative study is Harold Platt's *Shock Cities: The Environmental Transformation and Reform of Manchester and Chicago*. Manchester and Chicago make useful comparative case studies because they were both 'shock cities' during the Industrial Revolution, depicting, in a real and figurative sense, 'the horror and wonder of contemporary society on both sides of the Atlantic'. Utilizing new technologies of production and infrastructural systems, this engendered 'a new form of built environment' in both cities, 'whose patterns of land use, shapes on the ground, and social geography' added to their shock value and generated an unprecedented environmental impact on both cities' internal and external relationships. Engineers like John Frederic La Trobe Bateman and Ellis S. Chesbrough were the architects of nature, designing and executing ambitious sociotechnological infrastructures in order for their municipal employers to draw upon water to foster urban demographic growth. They were equally important in helping to sustain a city's metabolism and enable it to function organically; that is to say, by circulating the inputs of natural resources required by urban populations – air, water and food – for living on, while also aiding the outputs of waste products through sewage and refuse disposal. In so doing, men like Bateman and Chesbrough were integral players in transforming natural and built environments alike. As with the best urban history scholarship, then, Platt's study marries the case-study focus with the wider technological focus on the city-building process, bringing human and non-human drama into the narrative.[21]

Urban historians have long been interested in the built environment: studies have famously focused on the effect of cities' economic and social activities on both the natural environment and public health, via pollution of the air and waterways, as well as on interdependencies between humans and non-humans (horses, in particular, as a source of manual power and transportation) in shaping urban and suburban development, including commercial and other regulatory activities (with horse-drawn fire engines and ambulances).[22] Even more prominent in the urban history scholarship has been the role played by natural energy resources like water in allowing urban residents to perform everyday social and economic tasks, but also in improving public health and engineering urban spaces. Water has been a pivotal force in urban production, distribution and consumption, utilized as part of technology in bringing nature into the city for the benefit of mankind; it is integral to the construction, growth, health, materiality and governance of the city.[23]

Continued scholarly interest in urban water supplies also owes much to the recognition that water poverty remains a pressing concern in the world. Water is an important subject for historians interested in public safety in cities as well as public health, not least because it can cause widespread urban destruction – as seen in the recent cases of the 2004 Indian Ocean tsunami and the storm flooding of New Orleans in 2005.[24] Platt's study of Chicago and Manchester reveals the tensions evident in Victorian waterworks engineering, especially following the widely publicized failure of a dam outside Holmfirth, West Yorkshire, in 1852, which drowned eighty-one residents and caused considerable damage to property and infrastructure. Twelve years later, at the village of Low Bradfield outside Sheffield, South Yorkshire, a larger reservoir failure, involving upwards of 300 victims and thousands of pounds' worth of destruction across Sheffield and its hinterland, brought the issue of water governance, including the legal obligations of waterworks' proprietors, firmly into public consciousness. My own research into these floods reveals how threatening water could be to a city's residents and prosperity, but also how resilient communities were when faced with the destructive elements of nature.[25]

Baghdad, for example, has been flooded by the Tigris River many times throughout its long history – not to forget the recurring destruction wrought by warfare and plague – but continues to thrive as one of the largest and more significant cities in the Muslim world. Otfried Weintritt documents up to thirty-five disastrous floods of Baghdad from the beginning of the tenth century to the middle of the thirteenth century alone; floods were so common that contemporaries differentiated between 'normal' spring-time crises caused by annual high waters and '"abnormal" catastrophic floods' when installing flood-control systems such as dams and canals. The data was well documented by chroniclers for this period due to Baghdad's importance as a political and economic centre of Mesopotamia; as its importance declined between the thirteenth and nineteenth centuries, so too did documentary records of its floods.[26] This example and others reveal how the material, environmental, political and cultural meanings of water have attracted much recent interest, while also illustrating that the field of inquiry has steadfastly remained rooted on local case studies notwithstanding the gathering momentum to write global environmental histories.

From the City Sink to the City Monument

The search for a suitable source of clean water, its safe storage and the disposal of waste-water – or what Tarr calls 'the search for the ultimate sink' – started as a problem with a decidedly local focus: the majority of medieval and early modern urban water supplies were obtained from local wells or pumps, drawing from groundwater, rivers and streams, while waste (both human and manufacturing/commercial) was either disposed of in cesspools or dumped back into local rivers and streams. Too few towns supplied sufficient piped water in the early modern period; those that did only offered it to those who could afford it. Many residents relied on water carriers for supplies until the installation of steam pumps in the eighteenth and nineteenth centuries. Intermittent supplies of water of dubious quality created enormous public health problems, including low life expectancy, as cities and their populations were poisoned by their own waste products. Recognizing this, during the eighteenth and nineteenth centuries urban institutions – firms, charities, municipalities and even national governments – sought healthier and safer sources of water supply and the means of waste disposal.[27]

As Carl Smith's excellent comparative study of water-works projects in Philadelphia, Boston and Chicago demonstrates, this was an expensive and cumbersome search, fraught with technological and political disputes and set-backs. Early innovators, such as Philadelphia's Watering Committee, which constructed its own waterworks in 1802 to bring drinking water into the city from the Schuylkill River, soon found that their systems contained insufficient capacity to supply fast-growing populations. Philadelphia's response, to utilize steam engines to drain the river more efficiently, proved to be an expensive and unpopular solution for the city's tax-payers. It was not until the 1820s that a fairly efficient system of gravitational water engineering was introduced – this included moving the water intake upstream and building a reservoir on Fairmount Hill to impound it, as well as substituting iron for wooden water pipes to reduce leakage in the city – and it was another decade before the whole scheme proved to be financially viable. The natural environment had, for the time being at least, yielded to man's control and water consumption rose significantly. In fact, the whole experience placed Philadelphia at the forefront of waterworks technology and governance because it illustrated the advantages of having a publicly owned waterworks system, while also teaching valuable engineering lessons to other cities that were embarking on similar projects.[28]

Smith uses the idea of the 'urban water grid' to illustrate the blurred distinction between nature and the built environment. Industrial cities built expensive waterworks systems to improve the quality of life of their residents and protect property from the risk of fire, but also to celebrate their conquest of nature. These capital-intensive projects demonstrated cities' dependence on nature in a human-made world that was, paradoxically, increasingly detached from nature. Yet the building of a physical infrastructure – the reservoirs, towers, aqueducts, water pipes and faucets that brought nature into the homes and workplaces of city residents – was not the only impetus for such investment; city leaders and officials also built an infrastructure of ideas, utilizing water to glue disparate urban populations together into a cohesive community that collectively saw the public ownership of water as bringing 'comfort and health' to all. As Smith writes, a 'city is as much an *infrastructure of ideas* as it is a gathering of people, a layout of streets, an arrangement of buildings, or a collection of political, economic, and social institutions'. Thus, the interdependence of the natural and built environment is evident in the engineering of natural water sources – building reservoirs, engine houses and aqueducts gave city authorities control over their neighbouring watersheds, but not without, first, headaches over the best technological solution for rendering the natural environment subject to their control, and, second, legal and political conflicts over the ownership rights and funding of urban infrastructure, as well as levels of charging for usage. For the personalities involved, then, these projects revealed deep-rooted anxieties about the character of modern urban society, including 'the alterations that urbanization was working on the natural world, the health of the urban individual and of the city as a whole, and where their metropolis stood in the course of human events'.[29]

Smith's book continues an emerging trend in the literature to examine the materialism of the urban environment and its relationship to nature. This is partly the product of the cultural turn in history, under which nature is understood as a discursive product of social and technological forces, but is, too, a response to Worster's complaint that the built environment is wholly expressive of culture. It is also, as Chris Philo puts it, a reflection of the necessity for historians and geographers to pay closer attention to the '"thingy", bump-into-able, stubbornly there-in-the-world kinds of matter' that shape the rhythms and spaces of everyday life.[30] By revealing how nature came to be discursively separated from culture, Matthew Gandy, Maria Kaika and Zachary Falck, amongst others, have rematerialized the natural and built environments. In so doing, they draw upon the cultural geographer Erik Swyngedouw's concept of 'socionatures', which refers to the ways in which human and non-human agents constantly interact to produce the flows, movements and circulations that give cities material form.[31]

In *Concrete and Clay: Reworking Nature in New York City*, Gandy traces the extension of New York's water catchment area from the early nineteenth to the late twentieth century, taking in thousands of square miles of mountains, lakes and forests, villages and flood plains. Through the building of nineteen reservoirs, along with a supporting technology of tunnels, storage tanks and water mains, including the world-famous Croton Aqueduct, New York delivers 1.3 billion gallons of water every day to a population of approximately 9 million people. Gandy sums up the relationship between urban growth and water as being founded on the continuous interaction of the natural and built environments – the embodiment of 'socionature':

> The history of cities can be read as a history of water…To trace the flow of water through cities is to illuminate the functioning of modern societies in all their complexity. Water is a multiple entity: it possesses its own biophysical laws and properties, but in its interaction with human societies it is simultaneously shaped by political, cultural, and scientific factors.[32]

The building of the Croton Aqueduct between 1834 and 1842 'marked a new era in North American urbanization', one that was increasingly recognized for its public celebrations and a nascent civic pride. Moreover, the process of extending the city's ecological frontiers also marked the evolution of 'a new kind of technological and cultural engagement with nature…a democratization of nature'. Reservoirs and water pipes were joined by fountains and fire hydrants, which symbolized the arrival of a fresh and plentiful supply of water to the city together with a new understanding of public health and safety. This widespread availability of water in turn encouraged growing consumption, the diversification of water uses, the diffusion of plumbing technologies within the home, and the evolution of a new culture of personal hygiene. Gandy further comments how 'the growing use of water would [in time] be seen as an indicator of modernity' inasmuch as it marks the paradoxical nature of modernity; nature was both servant and master to New York in this narrative.[33]

As is often the case, cultural explanations can mask the lived reality of urban environmental change, which is why there has been a renewed interest in the materiality of urban environments. Fortunately, Gandy recognizes the pressing social and economic factors that forced the hand of New York's authorities to seek untapped sources of clean water during the 1830s and 1840s. These included an increase in water-related disease outbreaks across the city; escalating property damage from fire (including a 'great fire' in 1835 which destroyed 674 buildings); the growing professional status of engineers, who convinced the city's political and economic elites to seek 'a more technically ambitious solution to the city's water problems'; and lobbying from interested parties (chemical works, breweries, tanneries, insurance companies and the like) for more reliable water supplies for manufacturing and fire protection.[34] This emphasis on the traditional social and economic explanations, coupled with a renewed interest in material technologies, is commonplace amongst histories such as Gandy's and owes much to the traditional leanings of urban history scholarship; it is this combination of evidence and theory, presented in an inter-disciplinary framework, which has formed the bedrock of the field.

Standing at the Crossroads

In a survey article on recent PhD theses in urban environmental history, Stéphane Frioux warns that the field stands at a crossroads in its fledgling history. Since it stands 'at the intersection of various related approaches', there are multiple directions for its practitioners to take, notably in moving away from some of the well-trodden topics (pollution and public health, for instance) towards emerging issues such as environmental inequalities and social justice, but also to re-scale downwards from industrial metropolises on to smaller cities, and temporally away from the nineteenth century: either forwards into the twentieth century or further back in time to better understand how pre-modern communities coped with environmental crises. Additionally, there is an opportunity, as the urban economist Edward Glaeser argues, for cities to become the vehicle for environmental improvement; urban and planning historians clearly play an important role in highlighting the long-term context for this, as Sir Peter Hall's final book demonstrates.[35] New geographical vistas are equally welcome, not least because – as this chapter clearly demonstrates – the vast majority of published research has focused on North America and Western Europe, especially during the nineteenth century.

To move towards a global urban environmental history, we need to consider the built environment in Africa, the Middle East and Asia – not to forget other under-researched regions like Latin America or Eastern Europe. There are some positive signs that these omissions are being addressed, albeit currently in general environmental histories without the case-study focus.[36] Moreover, the historiography on natural disasters has paid close attention to cities in the developing world, partly because they tend to suffer from a greater number of catastrophes, but also because their experience reveals alternative strategies of coping with disasters. As Christof Mauch notes, 'how humans deal with catastrophes depends largely on social and cultural patterns, values, religious belief systems, political institutions, and economic structures'. Whereas few Westerners continued to interpret natural disasters as acts of God following the Enlightenment, disasters in China were seen as 'heaven-sent' until well into the nineteenth century, while Islamic societies understood catastrophes through a mixture of theology and technology. In other disaster-prone communities – like the Philippines and Mexico – the frequent experience of natural disasters and other crises helped foster a 'cumulative disaster knowledge' by which communities were better able to cope with the risks associated with urban life.[37]

Greg Bankoff's research into the urban fire regime of Manila, the capital of the Spanish Philippines, illustrates the varied cultural responses to natural disaster. In effect, Manila was two cities: a core walled city of stone and wood largely inhabited by Spaniards, and an outer city of nipa palm and bamboo houses, densely packed together and inhabited by the indigenous population, as well as Chinese and Japanese settlers. The stone and wooden city was built to repel, or at least contain, fire as well as earthquakes, whereas the highly flammable nipa-palm city was built with the recognition that periodic conflagrations were inevitable consequences of urban living; these houses were rebuilt almost as quickly as they burned. In this respect, outer Manila is similar to pre-modern Asian cities, where, as Lionel Frost argues, urban residents responded to the constant threat of fire by building houses cheaply with minimal furnishings. Since hazard was virtually an everyday life experience in the

Philippines, indigenous populations coped remarkably well with disasters, adopting a degree of fatalism, risk-taking and even humour in their attitudes towards hazard.

Bankoff demonstrates how this dual approach to planning and fire management in Manila first reflected ethnic divisions within the newly colonized state, before class distinctions further complicated matters in the nineteenth century. As Manila underwent a demographic surge following its growth as a trading port, stone-built houses spread amongst the nipa-palm ones in the outer city, new commercial and retail suburbs emerged to fuel this new wealth amongst some sections of the non-Spanish population, and organized fire brigades were established. For the colonial administrators, the protection of fixed property remained the driving force behind the spread of stone buildings, whereas the indigenous population prioritized rescuing their portable property, giving up their homes to the flames. There thus existed a 'fire gap' within Manila, which separated its inner core from its outer periphery, and revealed social and ethnic inequalities in its pyromorphology.[38]

This emerging research strand also reveals how fires and other disasters are deeply embedded in social and ecological structures and reinforce existing social inequalities. At its simplest level, wealthy Western societies are far better prepared for earthquakes than poorer developing societies. One estimate calculates that in Los Angeles approximately 50,000 people would be killed by an earthquake measuring 7.5 on the Richter scale, whereas a similar quake in Tehran would probably kill 1 million.[39] Yet there also exist clear social inequalities within Western societies: in Edinburgh's great fire of 1824 and San Francisco's earthquake and fire of 1906, properties inhabited by working-class households were at far greater risk of destruction than those in which the wealthier middle classes resided. The same logic applies to the flood victims of Holmfirth and Sheffield: the overwhelming majority of deaths affected working-class families, and the loss of property and employment was also felt most deeply by the poor. Similar conclusions are being reached across the spectrum of case studies and topics.[40]

If urban environmental history is standing at a crossroads, then, its prospects still look positive. It has achieved a great deal in broadening the methodologies at the disposal of urban historians as well as the all-round appeal of the discipline. It has introduced nature into historical studies of the built environment, reintroduced a sharpened focus on urban materiality, extended our focus on the city to consider its 'ecological footprint', and given urban history a new edge by introducing scientific and technological questions into the study of the city-building process. It also opens up wider audiences for urban historians – including practitioners, policymakers and the general public.[41]

Yet the relationship has been reciprocal and urban environmental historians recognize this: urban history has rooted environmental history in a long-established tradition of scholarship – many of the questions and topics that are scrutinized today can be traced back to the early years of urban history as seen in chapter 1. Moreover, cities continue to play a defining role in shaping the research agenda: their huge appetites for natural resources, given the large-scale demographic explosion of past centuries, has rendered the city the most important outlet for environmental historians, while urban ecologists, economists and planners continue to draw on urban histories to advocate citywide solutions to environmental problems. City case studies bring life to both fields: they expose the variety of attitudes and strategies for managing the natural and built environments; while comparative studies – which are growing in number and usefulness – continue to highlight the generalities and specificities of a city's experience for urban history. Emerging interest in understudied cities and regions of the world – coupled with a nascent global approach – continues this rich tradition.

5

Urban Culture and Modernity

In an essay published in 1938, Louis Wirth, the Chicago School sociologist, argued that modern cities were noticeably different from their pre-modern counterparts: they were larger and more densely inhabited, and also more heterogeneous in their demographic composition, with sharper degrees of socio-spatial segregation. The traditional basis of social solidarity provided by family and kin was being eroded by growing individualization and isolation within urban society, as well as the emergence of new forms of collective identity in the form of the club and voluntary association to counteract this. Urban dwellers, he wrote, depended on more people for their everyday interactions, but these were increasingly fleeting and segmented, which produced a series of impersonal and superficial exchanges between self-interested individuals, governed by contract rather than social custom.[1]

Wirth believed that, in order to advance our understanding of the modern urban condition, we needed to interrogate its spatial and experiential features. For Wirth and other contemporary writers like Max Weber, there was something distinctly 'modern' about the urban culture that they were describing. While there were a greater number of opportunities facing the individual in a modern metropolis like Berlin or Tokyo, the growing individualization of society produced a heightened sense of alienation between the urbanite and the city. Later writers, such as the cultural theorist Michel de Certeau, have shown how the way that a city is conceived by a planner or mapped by a cartographer – with its 'top-down' panoramic views, scaled distances, and clearly defined routes for vehicular and pedestrian traffic – is different from the way that the same city is experienced, or learned, by the walker, or, as in this author's case, the runner, who takes his or her own route – including undefined and unmapped 'short cuts' – *through* the city streets and alleyways, and experiences the city in a sensuous way, distinct from, yet related to, the planner's understanding of it. Individuals develop their own 'ways of operating' in everyday life, which allow them to reinvent a static space into a lived place.[2]

Since the cultural turn in the 1980s, there has been a growing trend within urban historiography to examine the spatial and experiential nature of the modern city in tandem. Urban histories have considered the juxtaposition between attempts by states and their agents to construct *and* regulate a built environment in their own image, and the life of the street 'from below' in which ordinary people, with a wide spectrum of social identities, experienced urban life. Along-side a recognition that the 'modern city' is largely a Western-constructed model – embodying an industrialized economy, new forms of commercial culture, a greater variety of regulated public spaces, and improved inter- and intra-urban communication, including mass passenger transport and a lively print culture – non-Western cities and urban cultures have, particularly since the second half of the nineteenth century, been brought into contact with Western values through the West's exporting of this model (sometimes forcibly). The same can be said about what Wirth described as an urban 'way of life', though what this means can easily be lost in translation, or adapted to suit particular cultural traditions and political agendas, as a diverse array of city-based studies have done. Non-Western cities have subsequently been interpreted as the locus for the struggle between the forces of modernity and national identity when new cities are built, or existing cities transformed, by modernization and nationalism. This chapter will consider the ways in which the forces of modernity – as a paradoxical embodiment of all that is simultaneously pleasurable and perilous about urban society – helped shape modern cities across a broad geographical vista.[3]

Modernity and the Built Form

The Marxist philosopher Marshall Berman famously defined modernity as 'a mode of vital experience – experience of space and time, of the self and others, of life's possibilities and perils...a maelstrom of perpetual disintegration and renewal that left no stone unturned'.[4] 'Modernity' is generally seen as the cultural manifestation of urban industrial capitalism, specifically of the homogenization of culture and its everyday practices. The term is often used interchangeably with 'modernization', taking on a new resonance by denoting a period of new or accelerated change: in economic and industrial structures, forms of production and consumption, demographic movements, communications, political forms, the arts and popular culture. Modernity thus has a paradoxical meaning, in encapsulating all that is ephemeral, transient and fleeting within society, as well as all that is rational, immutable and eternal. It subsequently helps to produce a new commodified world in which, to quote Karl Marx, 'all that is solid melts into air'.[5]

In an urban context, the experience of modernity is often discernible through the dialectical relationship between time and space. The city exemplifies modern life's possibilities and perils, and is both the embodiment of and an active participant in this maelstrom of perpetual change: constantly evolving in its form and function, subject to the forces of destruction and reconstruction, and the locus of struggle between the forces of modernization and preservation. Because of the influence of a number of European philosophical writers, including Charles Baudelaire, Georg Simmel and Walter Benjamin, urban modernity is most closely aligned with the emergence of the Western metropolis in the seventy years or so after the mid-nineteenth century. The capital cities of Paris, Vienna, London, Berlin and Budapest, as well as industrial cities like Manchester and Chicago, underwent major physical and spatial transformations, standing out as exemplars of progress and change, freedom and anxiety, especially around the *fin-de-siècle*.[6]

In *The City as a Work of Art*, Donald Olsen evocatively describes how Baron von Haussmann's demolition and subsequent reconstruction of the Parisian city centre during the 1850s and 1860s swept aside an 'old Paris' reviled for its 'dark, dirty, narrow streets', and arguably established its successor as the 'capital of modernity' by building broad, straight, tree-lined boulevards, bordered with richly ornamental and decorative mansions, cafés, theatres, concert halls, public monuments and public buildings. In so doing, the street was transformed into a site of bourgeois consumption, promenading and surveillance, thereby excluding large sections of the poor from the new centre. The construction of the *Ringstrasse* in Vienna after 1859 similarly replaced that city's walls and moats with a long and wide boulevard of civic and state buildings, opulent mansions, open spaces and the state opera house, which rivalled the grand boulevards of Paris in architectural grandeur and monumentality, and provided ample room for 'the pomp and spectacle' of the Viennese aristocrat.[7]

In his study of the public culture of the Victorian middle class in northern English cities, Simon Gunn locates the development of urban modernity in Birmingham, Leeds and Manchester in its architectural, spatial and representational form. It was not enough for cities to be rebuilt in stone and brick; they also had to be reimagined through print culture and the arts. The transformation of the central core of these cities into clearly defined city centres, with retail, commercial and civic spaces, recast them as spectacular examples of urban modernity where social identities were fashioned and framed. The building of town halls, railway stations, warehouses and department stores illustrated a wider shift in the industrial city's representation away from a place of manufacturing to a place of consumption and display. Embodying multiple architectural styles – neoclassical, Gothic and Italian Renaissance – their monumentality evoked images of wealth, spectacle and the sublime. Manchester's *palazzo* warehouses, built from the 1840s onwards, epitomized the ambition of that city's commercial elite, while a major public building drive from the 1850s onwards stamped the municipal authorities' ambitions firmly on to the landscape. As Gunn writes, these buildings 'did not denote nostalgia for the past or a retreat from the modern'; rather they were 'understood as fundamentally modern in their design, in their use of materials and the incorporation of the latest technical facilities'. For instance, the installation of expensive clock towers – famously with Cuthbert Brodrick's design for the Leeds Town Hall – asserted the importance of time discipline in the heart of the commercial city, but also established the monumentality of the town hall, with its tower sharing the city's skyline with factory chimneys and church spires, and symbolized a shift in power away from traditional institutions like the church towards secular ones like the democratically elected town council.[8]

Although modernization was a Western conception of urban planning, unsurprisingly, it generated imitations and new forms as it was exported around the world and adapted to fit the existing cultures of non-Western cities. European planning models, especially Haussmannization and the Beaux-Arts tradition, were highly influential in the development of Middle Eastern and Latin American cities, especially during the belle époque. Arturo Almandoz records how Haussmann's *grand travaux* in Paris became 'the main symbol of modernization imported by some Latin American capitals during their republican consolidation'. Haussmannesque boulevards and tree-lined avenues were cut into existing cities to transform them into spectacles of Western modernity: these included Paseo de la Reforma in Mexico City, Parque de Palermo in Buenos Aires, and Avenida Agraciada in Montevideo.[9]

Similarly, Ottoman engineers cut new boulevards and lined them with Western banks and department stores (including branches of famous European stores like Le Bon Marché and Steffl in cities like Cairo). They also installed new infrastructural amenities as part of the nineteenth-century *Tanzimat* (meaning 'reorganization') reforms in cities, which recognized the rise of a new urban middle class: these included improved passenger transport, public lighting, water and sewage, and the provision of more organized forms of 'respectable' leisure such as theatres, opera houses, horse tracks and parks, in cities ranging from Istanbul to Tehran.

Many new streets were named 'Rue de Rivoli' to denote their similarities to the Parisian original, and symbolized the improved circulation of goods, people and ideas. Symmetrical and regulated European-style public squares, flanked by public buildings and peppered with memorials to colonial rule, were installed across the French Maghrib and the Ottoman Middle East – from the Place d'Armes in Algiers (1830) to Al-Marjeh Square in Damascus (*c*.1866–84). Some clock towers, such as Beirut's (1897) at the Place Hamidiyyeh (later renamed Place de l'Union and, later still, Martyrs' Square), had multiple facades exhibiting different ways of time-keeping, including traditional alaturka time in Arabic and European alafranga time in Latin numerals. These demonstrated the imperial authorities' attempts to bring a secular order and discipline to the cities and their social practices as well as reflecting the cosmopolitan nature of modern urban identity. This long journey towards modernization along European models continued well into the twentieth century in many cases, especially with the state-sanctioned building of high-rise housing blocks, American-style skyscrapers and urban freeways to accommodate the fast-growing populations, motor cars and capitalist values in Istanbul, Cairo and elsewhere, with more recent transformations to the skyline of cities in the Middle East, such as Dubai, Abu Dhabi and Doha, during the late twentieth and early twenty-first centuries.[10]

The diffusion of a Western model of modernization is similarly discernible in Eastern European cities, notably Russia's imperial capital, St Petersburg. Founded in 1703 by Tzar Peter the Great, St Petersburg was a city with its eye trained westwards from the outset. With a population of nearly 1.5 million in 1900 and over 2 million on the eve of the First World War, St Petersburg was constantly being rebuilt in order to retain its 'magnetic power' (*pritiagatel'no znachenie*) to attract newcomers. During the nineteenth and twentieth centuries, the state employed Western-trained architects to build new streets and organize its public space in a style fitting for a European cultural capital. New commercial and cultural amenities, with the support of foreign capital, were added to existing streets. On Nevskii Prospect, 'the city's most important and symbolic street', the art nouveau Eliseyev

Emporium was built in the early 1900s, along with a reno-
vated Passage department store following its destruction by
fire in 1898, and a reconstructed Anichkov Bridge to accommodate the growing volume of vehicular traffic within the
city. New secular institutions for education and the arts were
established, while existing ones, like the Russian National
Library, continued to expand their collections; citizens were
cajoled into dressing in Western European fashions; while a
European-style police system was founded to ensure a well-
governed city. This new physical environment was, Mark
Steinberg writes, designed 'not only to represent a changing
Russia to the world but to effect change itself, including in
how people acted, thought, and felt'. This was particularly
important given the multinational composition of the city's
population: the 1897 census identified sixty ethnic groups
(based on language) living in the city, the vast majority of
whom were born in the Empire yet claimed a non-Russian
mother tongue.[11]

These examples illustrate the importance of the city centre
to modernity. This was a space 'at the heart of the city' where
different social types could meet and interact, bringing with
it a tangible sense of excitement as well as danger. It marked
out the main commercial and retail space of the city, as well
as civic space with its town halls, libraries, art galleries and
other public buildings. During the late nineteenth and early
twentieth centuries, city centres underwent redevelopment as
spaces for leisure, consumption and entertainment, the preserve of the wealthy elite or middle class; they were subsequently segregated spaces in both the cultural imagination
and the cost of the goods that they sold. Even though streets
like Nevskii Prospect attracted all types to stroll along the
pavements – Steinberg cites *flâneurs*, idlers, drunks, dandies,
prostitutes and the homeless, in addition to businessmen,
workers and respectable ladies – the vast majority were inevitably excluded from the elite properties that lined them,
owing to their poverty and supposed immorality.[12]

The city centre, then, was as much the creation of human
interventions, exclusions and attitudes towards consumer-
ism, segregation and planning as it was a product of economic forces and real-estate values. It was both a material
and an imagined space, and the recent historiography has

drawn on a rich variety of written and non-written records – fire insurance maps, directories, assessment rolls, business records, newspapers, postcards, photographs, film and personal testimony – to illustrate this, through studies of both individual building types (department stores or skyscrapers, for example) and whole districts. The focus has been on both the role of architects and property developers in designing and building these districts as well as the different ways that urban residents and visitors have experienced these new spaces and material technologies. A significant strand of the literature, as we have seen, focuses on the *fin-de-siècle* period at the turn of the twentieth century with excellent studies of, amongst other cities, Budapest, Vienna and New York.[13]

There is also a growing interest in post-Second World War building types – tower blocks, skyscrapers, luxury hotels, cinema multiplexes, even Cold War observation posts – and their connection with a modern globalized urban identity. Most ambitiously, the skylines of Dubai and Abu Dhabi, two of the richest cities in the world, have undergone remarkable transformations since the late 1990s by oil-rich billionaires. Aided by generous government support for development, as well as international investment, Dubai has been transformed into a glittering international tourist destination, while Abu Dhabi, with a population of approximately 920,000 in 2013, has been built upwards as part of its master plan, with a series of 'supertall skyscrapers' (including investment banks, five-star hotels, and mixed office and residential complexes like The Landmark and Sky Tower) across the city and its connecting islands vying for international attention. More modestly, perhaps, an old merchant and industrial city like Leeds is increasingly being referred to as 'skyscraper city' for its strategic development of tall buildings (including residential, educational and office developments) across a defined area of the city centre as a flagship component of the city's regeneration programme.[14]

There is also a growing connection between urban buildings and skylines and the wider geopolitical issues of security and international terrorism. The ideological battle in Cold War-era Berlin, for example, was played out through architectural competitions to dominate the city's skyline: the Fernsehturm (TV Tower, 1965–9), at 368 metres the city's tallest structure, and the Hotel Stadt Berlin (1967–70), at 125 metres the city's tallest building, both located on or near Alexanderplatz in East Berlin, symbolized East Germany's growing profile on a world stage. Contemporary New York, meanwhile, continues to be defined by its relationship to the World Trade Center, more than a decade after its destruction by terrorism, with commemorative histories, exhibitions and even popular films paying tribute to the lost icons of the New York skyline, as well as intense public interest in the subsequent plans to rebuild the Center's skyscrapers along with a national September 11 memorial. As the architectural historian Paul Goldberger makes clear, the Twin Towers, as they were popularly known, represented modernity 'and everything that modernity implies: choice, transparency, possibilities, and, most of all, the fact of constant change'. There is a clear consensus within this burgeoning literature that a city's identity is the product of its growth, and its changing function and use, and is intimately connected with particularly notable buildings and their continued existence in the popular imagination, even after their disappearance from the skyline.[15]

Taking a broad geographic approach, Alison Isenberg has convincingly shown how, in North American cities, downtown, in its early twentieth-century heyday at least, was not simply the linchpin of urban real estate and 'conspicuous consumption', but was also 'an idealized public place' produced and controlled through the prisms of class, gender and race. Isenberg examines the ways that downtown was culturally imagined in planners' reports and colour postcards produced by design consultants, stressing that these outcomes were often the response to the prevailing attitudes of consumers, business people and government leaders. Picture postcards of doctored 'Main Streets' provided beautified landscapes where 'hideous' or 'dangerous' material features (street utility poles, overhanging wires and other sidewalk obstacles) were removed, while aesthetic improvements were made to the street, such as the inclusion of paved sidewalks and illuminated store windows at night. Even with the subsequent 'decline' of downtown areas since the 1960s, accelerated by the upheavals brought about by rapid suburbanization, the growth of the motor car, racial tension, riots, and failed attempts at urban renewal, downtown subsequently became invested with a strong sense of collective, community-wide nostalgia for the loss of traditional department stores like Woolworth's, which further supports Isenberg's contention that downtown is both an economic and cultural artefact.[16]

City centres were also, increasingly, gendered spaces, as illustrated by the development of the department store, which created new commercial domains for middle-class women to shop, as well as economic opportunities for working-class shopgirls. Stores like Le Bon Marché in Paris, Whiteley's Emporium in London, Steffl in Vienna and Bloomingdale's in New York provided clean and safe environments within which women could actively participate within capitalist society. As influential studies by Judith Walkowitz, Lynda Nead and Erika Rappaport have shown, women were also co-producers of the new city centre, helping to transform it from 'a place traditionally imagined as the site of exchange and erotic activity, a place symbolically opposed to orderly domestic life' into a legitimate space of respectable leisure. Visiting these buildings and admiring the goods on display indicated an appreciation of modernity, while buying the goods provided full membership of the bourgeois club.[17]

The provision of new spaces for women was fraught with tension and anxiety, however. Rappaport cites moral opposition to William Whiteley's application for a licence to serve alcohol to his female customers, although this dissipated once his emporium had been established as a commercial boon to the area. Similarly, the provision of amenities aroused concern about the personal safety and morality of young female shoppers. Andrew May discusses how women were excluded from the early move to install public lavatories in Melbourne's principal streets, forcing them to use the facilities provided in tea rooms and department stores, which inevitably excluded many working-class women. Whereas the first male public urinals were opened in 1859, women did not get similar amenities until 1902, the same year as they got the right to vote and sit in the federal parliament. Even then, there remained a stigma attached to women being seen entering toilets in public. As May writes, 'The city was predominantly male space, and the ideological and actual separation of men's and women's roles was reflected not only in the extent of toilet provision, but in the spatial and temporal boundaries of those facilities themselves.'[18]

The Street as a Site of Modernity

The examples discussed thus far illustrate the ways that the street became a site for human drama, opportunity and conflict. Access to the street reflected and refashioned social identities as much as the buildings that lined it. The street itself could be an ideological battleground, engaging people from different backgrounds in a contest for rights. Indeed, the street's role as an agent for political and social conflict invariably reflects the paradoxical sense of freedom and danger that is ever present in definitions of urban modernity: to take but one example of many, when Cairo was ignited by rioters in January 1952, it took the burning of hundreds of buildings – bars, cinemas, restaurants, hotels and department stores, 'the very signs of an exclusive modernity unaffordable to the majority of Cairenes' – to bring an end to the parliamentary monarchy that had ruled Egypt since 1922.[19]

The street is the site where a way of life can be traced through the behaviour of a variety of marginalized social groups – street hawkers, prostitutes, vagabonds, gays – and those who are brought in contact with them, including police and municipal actors. Through the use of newspaper accounts and official documentation, urban historians have fleshed out individual experiences of streets and other public spaces, and shown how a variety of minority voices are traceable to a particular place and time. This was the case with late twentieth-century New York Avenue in Atlantic City, once a thriving tourist destination for well-to-do families, which, through a process of 'opportunistic reconfiguration' by the city's gay male community, was transformed from a decaying street into 'the most exciting and alive place in town' during the 1970s. A combination of legal and socio-economic factors had seen Atlantic City suffer under the throes of de-industrialization, but, in the growing emptiness left by the flight of middle-class families, businesspeople bought up cheap real estate and opened new gay clubs, restaurants, shops and hotels. 'Emptiness', Bryant Simon notes, 'created the social space for "outness"' and gave a greater visibility and legitimacy to the city's sexual geography.[20]

Yet the street is not static space; it too changes over time in its layout, function and meaning. Thus, New York Avenue's gay heyday was short-lived once Atlantic City's business and civic leaders embraced gambling as a solution to urban decline in the late 1970s and redeveloped the street as a casino destination. This was subsequently accelerated by the AIDS crisis of the mid-1980s, which refocused the gay scene away from public spaces like the bar on to private and domesticated spaces. In the void left, the developers quickly moved in. In addition to the slot machines and blackjack tables, each casino had its own bars, lounges, restaurants and hotel rooms designed to distract customers from leaving the premises. Many of the gay-oriented businesses that had thrived in the 1970s subsequently closed down as a new type of individualistic tourist flocked to the city. The street was noticeably quieter as gamblers 'drove their cars to town, parked in towering multistory [*sic*] casino garages, ate at casino buffets, drank in casino bars or on the casino floor, and then left town five hours later'.[21]

The example of New York Avenue is symptomatic of a wider discrepancy between the way that developers viewed the street and how it was experienced by residents. The modern city planner had a bird's-eye view of the street, seeing it as a conduit to aid the circulation of goods, services and people, rather than as a site for social life and traditional community relationships. Increasingly, many planners, influenced by the pioneering work of modernists like Le Corbusier and Frank Lloyd Wright, saw the street as an obstacle to circulation and a symptom of the modern city's sickness. They embraced the era of the motor car, building urban motorways/freeways, ring roads and multi-storey car parks to aid the motorist on his journey into and through the city.[22] This was as discernible in cities in the developing world, notably Kuala Lumpur, Bangkok and Mexico City, as it was in Western cities like Los Angeles, Milan and Bradford. The historiography has subsequently turned its attention to the politics of urban traffic planning, as well as the materiality of traffic lights, street signs and road markings. This 'traffic architecture' littered the streets, chiefly to speed up the circulation of motorized traffic. This has rendered the street more as a link between the motor car and the multi-storey car park, rather than a discrete space for everyday social and economic interaction.[23]

These technocratic elites formed what Christopher Klemek calls the 'urban renewal order' with their shared aesthetic preferences and expert professional networks. They embraced modernist urban planning as an international movement of ideas and practices, the seeds of which were sown in the interwar years with the emigration of eminent European architects and planners like Walter Gropius and Hans Blumenfeld to North America. Aided by federal policies on housing and road building, as well as local municipal support, they helped establish modernism as the dominant planning approach in the 1950s and 1960s. Modernism has subsequently been located in the classroom, the conference hall and the pages of the professional press as well as on the street: Ellen Shoshkes, for example, has mapped the movements of the British town planner, editor and teacher Jaqueline Tyrwhitt between Europe, Asia and North America, in order to trace her personal and professional influences over urban modernism.[24]

Yet this bird's-eye view of the street, as Jane Jacobs reminded us, did not take into account the lived reality of the street. With each redevelopment, the planner turned his back on the street in preference of the block – 'self-contained, separate elements in the city'. For the planner, the block was simpler to map and easier to police, whereas the street was an intrusive divider of areas. Despite this, however, the street, in its many guises, remained 'the significant unit' for '[u]sers of downtown' who, she controversially wrote, 'know very well that downtown needs not fewer streets, but more, especially for pedestrians. They are constantly making new, extra paths for themselves, through mid-block lobbies of buildings, block-through stores and banks, even parking lots and alleys.'[25]

The street, then, was increasingly shunted upwards and outwards on to the margins of the city – this inevitably meant that working-class neighbourhoods, including long-standing ethnic communities like Boyle Heights in Los Angeles, were bulldozed and entire populations relocated.

Urban historians have, for instance, explored how post-war British planners sought to replant the traditional residential street-as-social-space into new high-rise housing estates, albeit with a functional and utilitarian twist. Inspired by the architectural ideas of international modernism – specifically Alison and Peter Smithson's 'New Brutalist' vision of high-density exposed concrete structures, and Le Corbusier's earlier *Ville Contemporaine* (1922) – twelve-feet wide elevated street-decks, or 'streets in the sky', wide enough to fit a milk float or two mothers each with a perambulator, were designed into estates such as Park Hill in Sheffield and Hulme Crescents in Manchester in the 1950s and 1960s. The idea was to re-create a supposed lost world of sociable streets, of children playing in the open air while their mothers happily gossiped. It also introduced an alleged new scientific rationality into residential planning since it gave the planner greater control over human interactions with their new environments, rather than the unmanageable back alleys of the 'slum' that they replaced. 'Streets in the sky' were symptomatic of the biopolitical control of the planner: they subtly extended the principles of efficiency and uniformity into the social interactions of the estate. The high-rise estate, Matthew Hollow writes, embodied 'a technique of power designed not to impose a set of regulations upon the tenants but, rather, one designed to encourage them to perform in certain ways'.[26]

Yet, as subsequent studies note, these 'streets in the sky' suffered from chronic problems of vandalism, crime and lack of privacy. From their beginning, there was confusion over whether they were public or private spaces, which was heightened by the local police's refusal to patrol Park Hill's decks. Their layout and openness turned the walkways into uncomfortable wind tunnels, rather than friendly spaces to linger with neighbours. 'Streets in the sky' were subsequently transformed into symbolic sites of anxiety about the failures of state planning to provide adequate social housing. However, tenant dissatisfaction with the standard of housing, coupled with a growing awareness of their consumer rights, coalesced with the formation of tenant groups from the mid-1960s, which fought for greater participation in estate management, although there remained an underlying issue about whether local authorities saw participation in the same way, or used it as another means to control tenants.[27]

More widely still, community mobilization against the 'urban renewal order' sought to promote neighbourhood preservation against top-down government planning or gentrification (urban renewal involving the displacement of the occupying population and its replacement by a wealthier, normally white, demographic). Notable examples include the freeway revolts in cities such as Atlanta, Philadelphia, Memphis and Nashville, the proposed redevelopment of New York's West Village, where Jane Jacobs was a resident, the planned redevelopment of a chocolate factory in Cologne, and the housing reform campaigns organized by the *asociaciones de vecinos* in 1970s Barcelona. A whole new generation of grassroots activists from the working classes, new left students and trade unions had emerged, who fought the planners and civic officials for a greater degree of participatory planning in their neighbourhoods.[28]

If the street symbolized urban modernity, this is complicated by the case of cities in the developing world where streets were often late additions to new areas. Rio de Janeiro's stunning mid-twentieth-century growth, in which nearly 2,000 streets were added to the city's legal grid between the 1930s and 1960s, illustrates the sense of speed and turmoil that coloured urbanization there. But this is an official figure and does not take into account the many more miles of unregulated self-made streets that were added to the self-built communities outside Rio's official limits. More than half of the city's native Carioca streets remained unpaved in the early 1960s, while pavements were an unknown luxury in the *favelas*. Similarly, Shanghai's early twentieth-century shanty-towns lacked the space for streets: houses in Yaoshuilong, for example, were built without development controls, and any free space was soon filled with straw shacks; any remaining spaces served as narrow lanes, barely allowing two men to pass shoulder to shoulder.[29]

The colonial city illustrates the perils and promise of urban modernity through the stark inequalities in wealth between rich and poor. Historical interest in Mumbai/Bombay and Kolkata/Calcutta in India, Rabat in Morocco, or Cape Town in South Africa, coalesces around the late nineteenth- and early twentieth-century period when they were initially recognized as modern metropolises with a complex picture of the way in which urban modernity was stamped on to the spatial and imaginary landscape. As Preeti Chopra persuasively argues, Bombay was never built with a singular colonial vision in mind. Rather, it was envisioned and built through a joint enterprise of colonial rulers, European mercantile and industrial elites, European and Indian engineers and architects, and Parsi philanthropists.

Chopra discusses the fascinating example of Khan Bahadur Muncherji Cowasji Murzban (1839–1917), a native Parsi engineer who worked in the city's Public Works Department before he was appointed executive engineer for the Municipal Corporation of Bombay in 1892. She describes Murzban as part of a 'silent and usually invisible native majority that carried out most of the work in the construction of the public buildings and infrastructure of colonial Bombay'. Having been educated at the Indian Government's School of Engineering, Murzban became a 'successful intermediary' between metropole and colony, obtaining membership of the British Institute of Civil Engineers and the Royal Institute of British Architects. He also travelled widely across Europe in the mid-1870s, before returning to design several important public buildings in Bombay, including the State Record Office and the Byramjee Jeejeebhoy Paris Charitable Institution, although his work went unnoticed in the architectural press. Murzban, with his Western-inspired training and foreign travels, as well as his religious and philanthropic work for the local Parsi community, enjoyed a hybrid modernity, 'almost the same, but not quite'. In official photographs of the time, he was most recognizable by the ever-present feature of his turban.[30]

A similar 'hybrid modernity' is discernible in the case of Middle Eastern cities where, despite 'Haussmannism', most existing cities retained their sizeable historic cores. Strict zoning controls were adopted in the twentieth century to preserve the picturesque character of ancient native districts, while historic monuments were earmarked for preservation in Algiers, Cairo and Fez, amongst others. Madeleine Yue Dong has mapped out a similar concern for urban heritage in twentieth-century Beijing (or Beiping as it was renamed from 1928–49). Once the Nationalists had shifted the national capital to Nanjing, Beiping was rebranded in the early 1930s as a 'modernized metropolis of the world', with its rich heritage of architectural relics – old imperial palaces, city walls and gates, and former imperial gardens – as well as a wealth of historical libraries. A municipal plan was drawn up in 1934 to attract foreign tourists, which involved a programme of restoration and repair to make historic sites in the city accessible. A network of travel agents and guidebooks (in English, French and Japanese) was established to support this grand project, which was funded jointly by the municipal government, local merchants and the railway companies. While the plan was halted by the subsequent resumption of hostilities with the Japanese, followed by the Civil War, it does point to an alternative reading of urban modernity in which a city's heritage was deemed to be an asset for particular cities, rather than a symbol of backwardness.[31]

The Experiential Nature of Urban Life

Modernity, as we have seen, was never simply ingrained in the built form of the city; it was equally discernible in the cultural landscape of the city. The way that people experienced the city's streets and other public spaces was central to the fleeting nature of modern urban life. The modern metropolis was increasingly depicted as a spectacle that was best experienced by walking the streets – both the modern commercial streets of the city centre and equally so the dark, foreboding streets and back alleyways of the slum. Only then could the paradox of wealth and misery be truly appreciated by the individual. Walking the city thus allowed urban residents – such as the newly married Csorba couple in 1870s Budapest – to experience metropolitan culture in its widest scale: from watching fire-fighters risk their own lives to save the lives of others, to watching suicidal people render themselves temporarily visible to the crowd by jumping to their likely death from high bridges. That the Csorbas subsequently wrote up their experiences in their diary indicates the value of such events to their everyday lives and the ways in which a couple's public and private lives could overlap.[32]

The walker, or the *flâneur* as he is known in literary circles, is usually depicted in gendered terms as a male, upper-class agent of modernity who was able to freely enter and observe all areas of city life. He was first depicted as 'a person who walks the city in order to experience it' by the poet Charles Baudelaire, to refer to a class of male walkers wandering the streets of Haussmann's Paris. The term was subsequently coded in sociological and psychological terms by Simmel and Benjamin as the embodiment of a new, predominantly male, metropolitan state of mind characterized by boredom, idleness, distraction and feverishness regarding modern life. As a consumer of the spaces that constituted the city, he was both a detached observer of city life *and* a participant in its representation as gendered space. Simultaneously a man of leisure, freed from the pressures of work to explore the city, and an idler, lacking the responsibility of the working man, he was inevitably seen by some as a threat to existing urban relationships and social conventions.[33]

The majority of *flâneur*-types depicted by historians have tended to be writers themselves who reflected upon the dreamlike nature of modern city life, including Charles Dickens, Henry James, Hirade Kōjirō and Fedor Dostoevsky. Dostoevsky explored St Petersburg's landscape in 'the double role of *flâneur* and *feuilletonist*' by aimlessly wandering the city's streets as research for his newspaper columns and novels. He wrote about a 'sick, strange, and gloomy Petersburg', yet one that attracted people eager for life and hopeful of fulfilling their dreams. The *flâneur* has also been used to describe the work of journalists and social scientists who wrote exposés of urban life – W. T. Stead and G. R. Sims to name but two – a role which also included the growing army of anonymous journalists working for the daily newspapers being published in cities across the world.[34]

This reveals how the *flâneur* was not expected to walk unguided. The efflorescence of a mass newspaper industry, along with printed guidebooks and walker-friendly maps, aided him in his journeys around the streets. Modern metropolises like Berlin and St Petersburg depended on mass-produced newspapers, circulated throughout the city's central streets, which jointly produced and reflected the spectacle of metropolitan existence in an age of mass literacy. Multiple

editions of tabloid newspapers were published daily, embodying modern design techniques (bold headlines, large typeface,
scripted headers, and subheadings to break up the uniformity
of large columns of text), and providing material form to the
idea of the city 'as geographical place'. They offered a diet
of 'fleeting reportage' – feuilleton (gossip) sketches, short
stories, programmes of social events, and 'real life' eyewitness
accounts – that embodied the 'ephemeral quality' of modern
urban life. They also provided daily chronicles of incidents
on the city's streets – fires, tram accidents, rapes, stabbings,
arrests, etc. – including precise locations and times of the day
that such events occurred, which allowed the *flâneur* to locate
and visit such sites, thereby providing a material link between
the streets as physical and representative spaces.[35]

Studies such as these reveal how a variety of individuals
took an innate interest in observing and recording the
streets and people around them: journalists, novelists, artists,
photographers and film-makers alike. In Dziga Vertov's
superb documentary *Man With A Movie Camera* (1929), an
unnamed cameraman (Mikhail Kaufman) documents a 'day
in the life' of a typical Soviet city (the filming took place in
a variety of settings, including Moscow, Kiev and Odessa).
In a number of memorable scenes that play up the pace and
urgency of modern urban life, he films an onrushing train
from the tracks, races a galloping horse-drawn carriage, and
accompanies a fire engine as it rushes through the streets to
an emergency – the perils and dangers of the city are juxta-
posed against the thrill of the ride through the streets. The
audience is presented with an image of the perpetual motion
of street life, particularly as 'the city' awakens and the streets
come to life with throngs of people riding trams to work. A
series of shots of people entering and exiting revolving doors,
elevators and telephone kiosks represent the importance of
movement for a city, as well as its dependence upon modern
technology to regulate the increasing number of fleeting
social interactions. The relationship between the city and the
body (themes of hygiene, beauty and athleticism appear in
recurring scenes) is also explored, although here the cameraman's gaze is avowedly a male one, the identity of which is
constructed through the sexual objectification of women: the
camera candidly ogles a young woman dressing, lingering as

she fastens her stockings and bra; it later fixates on a woman's cleavage as she exercises on a rowing machine, and zooms in on numerous semi-clad and/or topless women sunbathing on Odessa's beach.[36]

Historians have gone on to challenge the normative identity of the male *flâneur* in recent years. We have already seen how women became actively engaged in the construction of particular spaces in the late nineteenth century. Judith Walkowitz has de-centred the *flâneur* and shown how, from the 1880s especially, new groups of women played increasingly important roles as urban walkers, spectators and consumers, especially across Western metropolises. These included those 'shopping ladies' discussed earlier who helped reshape the modern city centre; female music hall audiences and performers like Nellie Power (a male impersonator); charity workers and nurses who acted as a new type of 'urban explorer' in low-income residential areas; and the 'glorified spinsters' and 'New Women' who represented a new breed of working women who were independent enough to forge a life on their own without dependence on a male. Connected by drawing on the repertoire of the *flâneur*, these women established a new era of female participation in civic life based jointly on producing and consuming the modern city. We might also cite here various shots in Vertov's film – young Russian women working in the telephone exchange and the cigarette factory, having their hair and nails done in Western styles, or even staring back at the cameraman (and, presumably, the male viewer) from the Odessa beach – as evidence of newly empowered and independent women subverting the male gaze.[37]

Gay men, too, were able to subvert the *flâneur*'s normative (aka heterosexual) gaze by appropriating the social practice of wandering clearly defined spaces for their sexual pleasure. Various studies have demonstrated the importance of the design and layout of public space in constructing boundaries for non-heterosexual sexual encounters and in giving spatial expression to sexual minorities. As George Chauncey argues, public spaces – parks, beachfronts, washrooms and streets – were crucial for gay men who, in seeking same-sex relations, often had to escape the watchful eye of family and neighbours. Like the *flâneur*, gay men used a

variety of cruising tactics to move more or less freely around
public spaces like Central Park in New York, where they
could appropriate supposedly family-based spaces for themselves: these included the use of secluded spots and sub-
cultural codes like backward glances, the fixed gaze and
other seemingly everyday practices of initiating contact (such
as asking for a match or for the time of day in a particular
space).[38]

Commercial spaces could also offer sanctuary through
anonymity. For example, David Churchill discusses how
hotel bars in 1950s downtown Toronto offered middle-class
gay men the opportunity to meet each other in safety because
these were 'places a single man could go and not seem out
of place' during an era when gay men were regarded as a
threat to the social fabric built upon the nuclear family. The
obscurity of the crowd, the anonymity of the hotel bar, as
well as the cover of darkness provided by visiting a park to
procure sex at night gave gay men a degree of security, but
could also ramp up the danger of being arrested by under-
cover police officers or the threat of physical violence from
homophobes. This further illustrates how space is a constitu-
tive element of the cultural and social formation of metropolitan modernity. As Matt Houlbrook posits, '[m]ale sexual
practices and identities do not just take place *in* the city; they
are shaped and sustained *by* the physical and cultural forms
of modern urban life just as they in turn shape that life.'
While this meant that the city provided new opportunities
for sexual encounter and self-discovery, as Houlbrook illustrates through the story of Cyril L. – a young, anonymous
man who moved to London in the 1930s, where he discovered his sexual identity in the city's dance halls and Turkish
baths – it also meant sexual repression and intrusive policing,
as Cyril found when he was arrested for aiding and abetting
in keeping a disorderly house. Gay lives were shaped by the
contradictory experiences of love, sociability and citizenship
intermixed with fear, guilt and isolation; the city was equally
liberating and alienating. Despite the risks, however, 'privacy
could only be had in public' for men like Cyril.[39]

Tabloid newspapers also played a key role here in mapping
sites for same-sex sexuality and shaping public knowledge
about 'queer' life. Private details about Cyril were published

in tabloid newspapers to humiliate him and expose a dangerous underworld to newspaper readers. Yet Houlbrook simultaneously reads newspaper reports as suggesting 'how men
were able to create a place for themselves in the city and
explore how they understood and organized their desires'. In
his study of the tabloid geographies of gay male experience
in 1950s Toronto, Churchill similarly argues that, by providing 'a voyeuristic glimpse of transgressive sexuality' through
their regular reports on police arrests, as well as their gossip
columns, Toronto's tabloids utilized 'a camp code', which
familiarized readers with gay sites and acted as a guide for
gay readers keen to seek sex with other men.[40]

This chapter has discussed some of the ways that a modern
urban way of life has been mapped in histories of Western
and non-Western cities alike. It has revealed the paradoxical
nature of urban modernity as a tangible way of exploring the
physical/spatial and experiential nature of modern urban life.
The vast majority of published histories, as is the well-established tradition within the field, have taken the case-study
approach in examining the construction of the modern city,
and the role played by individuals – notably the *flâneur* in
his/her multiple guises – in moving around it, with varying
degrees of freedom. Surprisingly, there have been few explicitly comparative studies, although a number do situate their
cases within a broadly comparative framework (specifically
those which explore the adoption of Western models of urban
planning in cities in the developing world). It would be interesting to learn more about the ways in which the cultural
landscape of the city has been constructed through comparative studies, especially those which examine the types of
language used in reporting on modern life. A cross-national
comparative study of newspaper reporting on everyday life,
for example, would be most useful for revealing whether
there was a common language for understanding the city.
Further studies of small towns and provincial cities would
also add to our existing knowledge of modernity, which is
limited to large metropolises and capital cities; alternatively,
an examination of the way that a metropolitan modernity
was adopted, adapted and resisted by provincial cities could
reveal interesting insights about non-metropolitan forms of
civic identity.

6

Transnational Urban History

The rise of transnational history since the 1990s has responded greatly to what the sociologist Ulrich Beck famously described as 'a new dialectic of global and local questions which do not fit into national politics'.[1] Rather, research has sought to locate and trace the 'mobile subject' within global flows and movements since transnational studies, as a fundamentally transdisciplinary subject, has an intrinsic interest in the process of movement and the creation of what Arjun Appadurai, the anthropologist, has called the 'space of the flows' between nations.[2] The urban ethnographer Michael Peter Smith prefers to use 'translocal' to denote the multiple connections between different social actors across their departure, holding and destination points, further noting that transnationalism is a multidimensional process of movement, motives and interfaces, which takes place 'from below' as well as 'from above', and which involves local actors (human and non-human, including cities), cultures and identities that produce hybrid social and cultural practices. Smith also recognizes the importance of historicizing transnational practices because it illustrates the longer-term continuities in power relations between and within nation-states and local communities, while simultaneously reminding us that transnationalism is a recurring feature of modern life, rather than a recent by-product of neoliberal globalization.[3]

Cities and towns have historically competed with one another, especially since the emergence of nationalist movements from the eighteenth century onwards, but they have also increasingly cooperated through formal and less formal treaties, alliances and networks. There has been a collective sharing of knowledge and experience about the effective ways in which society can be governed. And while the world continues to be defined by nation-states – particularly in an age of domestic political retrenchment from Western states threatened by the challenge of emerging world powers like China, Brazil and India – such interconnections will remain secondary to the national problems, national solutions and national aggrandisement that national politicians consider to be most important. Yet as the political scientist Jeffrey Sellers reminds us:

> However globalized the world is, the local generally remains the level of analysis that is the closest to individuals. The effective character of policy, the dynamics of markets and class formation, the opportunities for political and civic participation, and the everyday constitution of identities all need to be analyzed at this micro level to be fully understood.[4]

A transnational approach to urban history complements the themes already explored in this book: it helps create social identity, generate new systems of governance, disseminate modern modes of thought and culture about urban planning, architecture and an urban way of life, and share environmental best practices. As the newest and least-developed subfield of urban history, it is likely to exert significant influence over the next generation of scholarship. This is because it helps explain the manifestation and spread of innovative practices, technologies and a creative class of urban professionals (scientists, engineers, designers, planning consultants), as the growing literature on creative cities shows.[5] Its very indeterminacy as a subject located at the interstices of multiple disciplines – anthropology, sociology, economics, political science, geography and so on – makes it a natural bedfellow for urban historians who are themselves at home with forging connections across the different fields of historical research. Transnational history further establishes the importance of comparative methodology, while also encouraging historians to get involved in cross-national, collaborative and interdisciplinary research activities, including conferences organized by international societies like the European Association for Urban History (EAUH), the Society for American City and Regional Planning History (SACRPH) and the International Planning History Society (IPHS). After tracing the meaning and evolution of the transnational turn in historical research, this chapter will then discuss some of the ways in which urban historians have utilized transnational approaches in their research, focusing mainly on the urban planning historiography, where there is a strong tradition of interest in the transnational circulation of ideas and influences.

Thinking about Transnationalism

A transnational turn is, by its nature, speaking to a committed following amongst urban historians because both approaches seek an alternative locus of historical interest, away from but connected to the nation-state. Neither involve what Sellers ambitiously dreams of, the entire replacement of the nation as the unit of analysis, because that would be a futile exercise in a discipline that has been so heavily shaped by the rise of the modern nation-state and the interconnectedness between city and nation over the last few hundred years. Sam Bass Warner, Jr, recognized this in the early 1970s, proclaiming that, 'Our urban history is the history of the conflicts and possibilities wrought by the growth of the nation and the growth of the units of its organization. It is also a history of the increasing interconnectedness of these units, which stems from the development of the economy and its cities.'[6] Although he was explicitly referring to the contemporary and historical experiences of Chicago, Los Angeles and New York, Warner's comments echo a widely held consensus amongst urban historians. As Pierre-Yves Saunier, one of the leading scholars in transnational history, eloquently puts it, 'History...has been the handmaiden of the nation-state for too long for historians to bluntly disregard the national frame.'[7]

Yet to strip away at wholly national explanations for historical change and look for varieties of experience within and between countries is increasingly useful for explaining the growing connections and entanglements between different peoples, ideas, commodities, cultures and places, which move across the traditional social, economic and political boundaries established by mainstream history. Though some historians prefer the labels 'world history' or 'global history' to explain their comparisons, transnational history seeks something different from these macro-historical approaches. Rather than assessing historical change across the global stage, a transnational approach seeks to map out and explain the spaces – and those who inhabit them – between and within countries, regions and localities around the world. Its application allows the historian to consider the relationship between the local, national and regional scales in explaining historical processes, including the formation, constitution and interaction of institutional networks and the spread and flow of ideas and ideologies. As Saunier and Akira Iriye put it:

> We are interested in links and flows, and want to track people, ideas, products, processes, and patterns that operate over, across, through, beyond, above, under, or in-between polities and societies. Among the units that were thus crossed, consolidated or subverted in the modern age, first and foremost were the national ones, if only because our work addresses the moment, roughly from the middle of the nineteenth century until nowadays, when nations came to be seen and empowered as the main frames for the political, cultural, economic and social life of human beings.[8]

This quotation illustrates some of the implied confusion about the definition of transnational history, as well as its theoretical and methodological variations. Some historians have clumped 'transnational' and 'international' history together, in much the same way that others see 'global' and 'world' history as the same subject. Yet others claim that the transnational approach was coined to distinguish the field in between nations from international history, which remains 'the study of nation-states interacting as such'.[9] In a special 'conversation' on what was then a fledgling subject in the *American Historical Review* in 2006, six historians debated the meaning and value of transnational history for historical research. In it, Christopher Bayly considered 'transnational' to be 'a restrictive term' for explaining historical processes before 1850 where large areas of the world were dominated by empires, city-states and diasporas rather than nation-states. Other contributors were more relaxed about using the term in a comparative setting, and over a longer-term framework, in order to understand earlier situations and processes that were analogous to those we understand today. Patricia Seed, for example, declared transnational history as useful for comparing movements of groups, goods, technology and people across time as well as in between spaces. Transnational history is, therefore, an approach that is both historically and geographically relative and, much like urban history, is interested in the creation and use of spaces to structure and represent human behaviour.[10]

Transnational history's older siblings – world and global history – have themselves been subject to much discussion; the former being an out-growth of the long-outdated area studies, while the latter's political roots are related to the rise of globalization studies amongst economists and political scientists since the 1970s. Sven Beckert, who has well-established credentials within urban history, persuasively argues that global, world, international and transnational history share more in common than they contrast: 'They are all engaged in a project to reconstruct aspects of the human past that transcend any one nation-state, empire, or other politically defined territory.'[11]

This early definitional confusion has been abated somewhat with the emergence of empirical histories. As an increasing number of historians have embraced these hybrid spaces in their research, transnational history has become more recognizable as a subfield of historical inquiry. It has equally become entangled with existing, long-standing fields like urban history. Historical journals have recently published special issues dedicated to urban transnational themes, urban studies journals have taken a more overt interest in historical case studies as well as international networks in their historical context, and academic publishers have dedicated entire book series to the area. The conferences of the EAUH and others regularly contain panels devoted to transnational, international and global topics.[12] There is now a regular and fertile exchange between urban and transnational history, so much so that it is impossible and unnecessary to distinguish between the two fields.

Locating the Transnational Variable in Urban History

Planning historians have had the most fruitful experiences with taking a transnational approach to their studies and there is a rich literature on the history of international exchanges in modern planning. There are three main areas in which this historiography has benefited from a transnational approach: first, the rise of an international planning associational culture in the years leading up to 1914; second, the revival of this culture in the decades after 1945; and, third, the relationship between urban planning and the colonial and post-colonial state in the twentieth century. This literature is, by its nature, comparative and diachronic in its approach; it is also interdisciplinary, involving conversations between historians and practising planners, and there is much overlapping interest between the scholarly and professional associations and their periodicals.[13] In so doing, planning historians have taken their cue from the pioneering work of Sir Peter Hall and Gordon Cherry, whose earlier studies of the ideological, intellectual and practical influences on the modern planning movement established the importance of considering the history of urban planning from its international as well as its local and national roots.[14]

Historical interest in the decades around the turn of the twentieth century has been sustained since the 1980s because, as we saw in chapter 1, this coincided with the urbanization process first attracting the systematic interest of municipalities, scholars and practitioners in the embryonic planning movement. Faced by a plethora of new or intensified challenges and opportunities – in the provision of public services, infrastructure or the maintenance of a decent quality of life for their citizens in an age of mass urban politics – city governments became recognizably more scientific and bureaucratic in their approach towards urban governance, hiring an ever-growing number of technocrats to manage the urban environment. By 1910, this had led them to build an increasing number of horizontal relationships with other towns and cities as part of an 'international milieu' of urban planning: these were organized around a variety of one-to-one exchanges of information, participation in one-off or recurring international congresses and exhibitions, and the development of dense networks of international institutions with subscription members, organizational committees, periodicals and annual conferences.[15]

Helen Meller, in her excellent study of the shaping of the European built environment, argues that 1890–1930 was a transitional period between a diminishing past in which cities grew organically with little effective regulatory control and a future in which 'new bodies of professionals, bounded by national legislation and informed by the international exchange of ideas, would be responsible for the quality of life'. She traces the growing influence of these new bodies through various comparative studies, including the provision of cultural institutions and exhibitions in the port cities of Hamburg and Marseilles, the provision of physical infrastructure in the Central European capitals of Budapest, Prague and Vienna, and working-class housing development in interwar Lyon and Birmingham. Together, the case studies reveal the interplay of local, national and international architectural, planning and civic traditions in producing variations of European modernism. Thus, the Villeurbanne and Kingstanding estates were built in Lyon and Birmingham respectively during a period of unprecedented economic and political crisis, where the provision of planned working-class housing had become a pressing matter faced by national as well as local governments, but both took markedly different physical forms owing to the varied national and local traditions of housing density, building materials, technology, party politics and greenfield development. As Meller concedes, while improved communications meant that 'ideas could be shared on a national, even international basis...this did not lead to any kind of uniformity of response. The utter contrast between Kingstanding and Villeurbanne demonstrates the importance of history, the cultural context and politics in determining the outcome.'[16]

More recently, there has been a heightened interest in the post-Second World War history of planning exchanges, especially (but not exceptionally) between Europe and North America. After the destruction of the war, planners across Europe faced the task of rebuilding damaged urban landscapes during a period of austerity, while also working in a new geopolitical environment marked by the Cold War and the birth of international institutions like the United Nations. Ideological influences came to bear over planning design and construction, especially in Berlin, which became an ideological front in redevelopment for Western and Soviet planners alike. A variety of transatlantic exchanges took place between Western-trained planners, politicians, scholars and other design professionals – otherwise known as the 'urban renewal order', which we have already encountered in earlier chapters – about the best way to modernize cities and adapt them to a global capitalist economy and the age of the automobile. These exchanges were, as various studies have mapped out, based around a combination of formal-institutional and informal-personal networks, drawing in a variety of 'big-name' planners – José Luis Sert and Le Corbusier to name but two – and lesser-known individuals like the British planner, editor and educator Jaqueline Tyrwhitt, who used her quiet, personal influence over Sert and others to encourage a decentralized and cooperative approach to international planning in a variety of male-dominated arenas, including the classroom and the planner's office. Other exchanges were coordinated by the institutional matrix of international associations, the regular meetings of which provided a well-established forum for the sharing of ideas and practices via such influential organizations as the Congrès internationaux d'architecture moderne (founded 1928), the International Federation for Housing and Planning (1913) and the Union Internationale des Villes (1913).[17]

Planning history has also recently converged with the history of imperial connections, not least in highlighting the hybrid cultural traditions and planning conventions that have emerged in the colonial and post-colonial world (see chapter 5). This emerging literature reminds us that transnational exchanges did not simply adhere to a donor–recipient metropole–colony model.[18] Recent research into the Ottoman Empire, for instance, illustrates how municipal and planning networks extended far wider and deeper beyond conventional centre–periphery imperial connections; local planning cultures slotted into the legislative framework devised in Istanbul to produce diverse outcomes in the built environments across the North African Mediterranean coast. For example, Zeynep Çelik and Nora Lafi have both shifted historical focus away from the imperial authorities' top-down missives on to the local and regional impulses that equally shaped the planning and development of provincial Ottoman and Maghreb cities, drawing on official archives as well as cultural artefacts such as photographs, written texts and paintings. They explore both the local and international circulations of influences on urban planning and building projects, and stress the cosmopolitan nature of Islamic urban modernity.[19]

Elsewhere, Nancy Kwak's study of planning and housing in post-Second World War Singapore reveals multiple local, national and imperial cultural interests and legacies, combined with transnational influences through international non-governmental organizations (INGOs) like the International Labour Organization and the United Nations' Development Programme over the city-state's nascent Housing and Development Board. Kwak describes a 'hyperconscious' sensitivity amongst Singapore's planning elites during the 1960s and 1970s, alert to Britain's new towns policies as well as emerging North American urban-renewal programmes, which were adopted as part of a 'patchwork' approach to national policy, 'where international best practices were patched together and assimilated with local needs'.[20]

Latin American planning has also attracted growing scholarly interest. Most notably, Arturo Almandoz has traced the Western influence over Venezuelan planning back to the sanitary reform years of the 1880s to 1910s. During the 1880s, Venezuelan delegates attended international sanitary and hygiene events in Washington, DC, Rome and Paris, which influenced a wave of medical education, governmental regulation and professionalization of municipal services in the capital city of Caracas during the 1890s and 1900s. This

culminated in a merging of public health and policing priorities when a 1910 ordinance established a city-wide legal
framework under which Caracas and other Venezuelan towns
with more than 1,000 inhabitants would be governed. These
earlier 'local' reforms, in which urban reform was under-
taken in a piecemeal and fragmented fashion, eventually
coalesced into a single 'macrocosmic or global vision of the
whole city' in the 1930s as the political and administrative
elite of Caracas embraced comprehensive Western-style redevelopment related to garden-city planning, through its Plan
Monumental de Caracas (1939).[21]

This fusion of local, imperial and extra-imperial influences
can also be traced in the movements of urban actors through
the transnational spaces in between cities. To take one
example, John Griffiths has meticulously studied the travels
and correspondence of Australian and New Zealand municipal officials between the 1890s and 1930s, tracing the early
ad hoc connections that existed within and alongside the
British Empire through the pages of the British world periodi-
cal, the *Municipal Journal*. Reports on overseas visits, observations and innovations – as well as job advertisements and
correspondence – illustrate how interconnected the *Municipal Journal's* readers were to the wider municipal world. New
Zealand's town clerks were just as interested in collecting
information and ideas from non-British sources as from the
metropole. Moreover, the varied geographical spread of such
publications reveals a convergence of urban, national and
imperial identities around the turn of the twentieth century,
and illustrates how there was 'at no stage a limited "one-
directional" flow of knowledge from Britain to the outer
reaches of the empire'.[22]

In situating their case studies in the decades around the
turn of the twentieth century, many of these recent studies
acknowledge and expand upon two exceptional works, Marjatta Hietala's *Services and Urbanization at the Turn of the
Century: The Diffusion of Innovations*, and Daniel Rodgers's
Atlantic Crossings: Social Politics in a Progressive Age. Published in 1987 and 1996 respectively, both studies were formative in shaping the subsequent relationship between
transnational and urban history, and illustrate how social
and municipal reforms were international phenomenon

subject to growing opportunities for transnational crossings in the decades leading up to and throughout the twentieth century. Furthermore, they equally challenge the traditional argument that the historical experiences of nation-states are exceptional. Both take their study of ideas, ideologies, tools, individuals and institutions to the international level and, moreover, interrogate the journeys and crossings that these involved, and not just their points of departure and arrival. They reveal how progressive reformers encountered a wide array of professional ideas and expertise in their crossings, as well as a plethora of types of services – planning, infrastructure, municipal enterprises, social insurance and modernist architecture – which fed back into their reports and policies. Foreign models and innovations never simply materialized as static things; they were the product of painstaking research and collaboration over time and across space by individuals and institutions, and were subsequently imported and exported according to a variety of local, national and even occasional international priorities. As Hietala herself concedes, in drawing heavily on the work of the sociologist Everett Rogers, '*An innovation is the general acceptance and implementation of new ideas, processes, products or services* [her italics],' which contains within it the capacity to change, as well as to be diffused through various channels of communication. To aid the spread of an innovation requires open communication channels, a sufficient – though not significantly delayed – time lag and an interconnected social system to pool together human resources and capital. Hietala's research historicizes this model in the context of transnational intermunicipalist exchanges amongst Scandinavian, German and British towns and cities.[23]

Hietala's and Rodgers's studies are further connected in examining the individual capacity and willingness to study and learn from overseas examples, thereby revealing some of the complexities of urban reform processes.[24] Rodgers reveals how, between the final quarter of the nineteenth century and the first third of the twentieth, a growing tide of North American social reformers, journalists and tourists visited European cities to study the organization and practice of municipal government there. The North Atlantic was the information superhighway of its age, teeming with 'cosmopolitan progressives' like Albert Shaw, George Parker and Julian Ralph, eager to digest the veritable cocktail of practices and infrastructure that had been innovated by European municipalities, which could then be translated into the American municipal system. This social exchange was predicated on the 'rapidly convergent economic development of the key nations of the North Atlantic basin...Nothing was more important for sustained trade in social policies than this dramatic expansion of the social landscapes of industrial capitalism.' Coupled with the growth of the nation-state and the recognition that the twentieth century was destined to be a universal urban age, the forging of these 'transnational social-political networks' vanquished any lingering remnants of either the 'real' or 'imagined' distance between these two continents. In this sense, Rodgers assesses the role of the nation in the transnational landscape, while simultaneously challenging the long-standing belief amongst many historians that North America enjoyed an exceptional status removed from the social upheaval and authoritarianism of European nations. Rodgers challenges this nation-centred simplicity and places the history of the United States' social policy and urban planning firmly in its international and transnational milieu; his work has subsequently gone on to significantly influence a new generation of doctoral and post-doctoral studies of the international circulation of the 'urban renewal order' across twentieth-century Europe, North America and Asia.[25]

Albert Shaw was one such transnational tourist. Having been schooled in sociology, and subsequently trained as a journalist, Shaw visited Europe in 1888 to study and report back on the practices of municipal government. He wrote about his observations in a two-volume study, published in 1895 while he was editor of the *Review of Reviews*. Like other American municipal tourists, Shaw was particularly struck by the 'businesslike straightforwardness and simplicity' of British municipal government, epitomized by the manufacturing cities of Birmingham, Glasgow and Manchester, each of which received a separate chapter in *Municipal Government in Great Britain*. Each city was noted for its specific innovations: Birmingham in gas and water utilities, Glasgow in gravitational water engineering and tramways, and

Manchester for sanitation, which captured the attention of curious travellers keen to learn and adopt new methods of municipal control. Notwithstanding their specialisms, however, Shaw identified that British municipalities, as we saw in chapter 3, were linked by a long tradition of local autonomy with functional and administrative decentralization, as well as clear legal rights and obligations, which helped to maintain a good degree of transparency in municipal affairs not readily recognizable on the continent.[26]

By devoting an entire volume to the British municipality, rather than incorporating it into his separate volume on the continental experience, Shaw sharply differentiated between municipal government in Britain's manufacturing cities and the European municipal system. As the first to do this, Shaw thereby established British urban politics as an exemplar of municipal government, and the comparative method as the best way of highlighting useful differences in practice. Shaw particularly stressed the merits of comparative method for American observers in enabling them to scrutinize British municipal institutions, particularly in the manufacturing towns, which he deemed worthy of comparison with similar-sized American industrial towns. To satisfy the American visitors' appetite for technical and scientific information on the practical workings of tramways, the finances of utilities, the coordination of the committee system of municipal government, and, more generally, the professionalization of municipal officials, he was expected to turn first to the British manufacturing cities before turning his attention to the continent for a comparison of municipal progress. Shaw's work subsequently went on to influence later advocates of the comparative municipal method, notably the British transnational local government expert, George Montagu Harris, who devoted his career to furthering the cross-national study of local government across a dense range of professional, public, academic and personal institutional networks.[27]

Hietala's study, too, focused in part on the British system of municipal government, but here the British authorities became the pupils, while continental authorities, particularly those in Scandinavia and Germany, provided tutelage. Whereas sporadic examples of municipal cooperation amongst British, German and Scandinavian municipalities existed from the 1860s and 1870s (she cites, for instance, Swedish and Finnish fascination with British earthen waterworks), the turn of the twentieth century saw new interest in cross-national municipal collaboration, especially in the fields of public energy, transport and planning. Periodicals like the *Municipal Journal* reported frequently on the examples offered by German municipalities in their prudent management of municipal services, politicians debated the finer details of the management of municipal services on the continent, while voluntary civic associations scrutinized the plans of overseas towns. For example, the British Committee for the Study of Foreign Municipal Institutions organized various visits, usually comprised of mayoral delegations, to Germany, Switzerland, Scandinavia and the United States during the 1900s. Their visits brimmed with fact-finding excursions to a variety of sites, including gas and electricity works, municipal schools, fire stations, old people's homes, poor houses, hospitals, baths and slaughterhouses, while their reports boasted of the value of first-hand observation, more efficient standards of public administration, improved public satisfaction with services, and, in a vain effort to advance the cause of Anglo-German relations during a period of heightened international tension, 'expressions of peaceful cooperation'.[28]

Our traditional picture of a centre–periphery model of innovations is, again, challenged by a plethora of interpersonal and inter-institutional criss-crossings, which link cities and countries that have been historically straitjacketed into simplistic developmental models: innovator and follower, donor and recipient, centre and periphery are all shorthand variations of this traditional approach. As Hietala succinctly puts it, nearly all towns and cities perform, at various times and across different channels, as receivers, generators or followers of innovations, while the channels that linked Scandinavia with Germany, Britain and elsewhere formed 'a complementary and interrelated whole, which changed and developed along with technological development and progress'.[29] Ultimately, this depended on a variety of complementary material: personal contacts, study tours, periodicals, comparative statistics, congresses and exhibitions, and was the product of specific local, regional and national municipal traditions, legal systems and cultures. The acquisition of knowledge combined with the building of contacts and relationships across national borders to make such connections useful exercises in the practice of policy learning as well as the evolution of administrative science.

In conclusion, there are positive signs that urban historians are continuing to roll back the institutional frontiers in their research to reveal the multiple motives and outcomes of the different actors, human and city, which make up these international networks. The richest and most insightful urban transnational history has done just this; urban historians like Hietala, Rodgers and Saunier combine structural explanations for historical change with a keen eye on the individual and the case-study approach. As argued in this and other chapters, urban histories, whether they take a comparative or a biographical approach, are at their strongest when they examine the relationship between space and place and, in so doing, reveal the roles played by people (whether these are local politicians, officials, employers, trade unionists, planners, builders, landlords and tenants, and so on) and their relationships with the town or city as a whole. It is axiomatic, therefore, that the chief advantage of taking a transnational approach within urban history is in enabling further interrogation of the connections between people and urban places – in their real and imagined senses – and in extending this lens outwards into a web of international, global and transnational connections; that is, of surveying the relationship between people, place and the spatial flows in between them.

Notes

Introduction: Why Urban History?

1   A reader looking for a comprehensive history of the urban world and the 'rollercoaster' ride of urbanization should start with Clark, P. (ed.) (2013), *The Oxford Handbook of Cities in World History* (Oxford: Oxford University Press). For urban histories of specific regions in the world, see Clark, P. (2009), *European Cities and Towns 400–2000* (Oxford: Oxford University Press); Pinol, J.-L. (ed.) (2003), *Histoire de l'Europe urbaine* (Paris: Seuil); Heitzman, J. (2008), *The City in South Asia* (Abingdon: Routledge); Jackson, K. and Schultz, S. (eds) (1972), *Cities in American History* (New York: Alfred Knopf); Freund, B. (2007), *The African City* (Oxford: Oxford University Press); Gilbert, A. (1998), *The Latin American City* (London: Latin America Bureau Press); El-Sheshtawy, Y. (ed.) (2008), *The Evolving Arab City: Tradition, Modernity and Urban Development* (London: Routledge).

2   Corfield, P. (2013), 'Conclusion: Cities in Time', in Clark (ed.), *Oxford Handbook*, 828–46, quote at 828. On the value of comparative methodology for history, see Sewell, Jr, W. (1967), 'Marc Bloch and the Logic of Comparative History', *History and Theory* 6: 208–18; Tilly, C. (1996), 'What Good is Urban History?', *Journal of Urban History* 22: 702–19.

3   United Nations (2013), *State of the World's Cities 2012/2013: Prosperity of Cities* (New York: Routledge), 25, 29, 30; United Nations Department of Economic and Social Affairs

(2014), *World Urbanization Trends: The 2014 Revision* (New York: United Nations Department of Economic and Social Affairs).

4   United Nations (2008), *State of the World's Cities 2010/11: Bridging the Urban Divide* (London: Earthscan), quotes at viii, xix; Warner, Jr, S. B. (1972), *The Urban Wilderness: A History of the American City* (New York: Harper & Row).

5   Chandler T. and Fox, G. (1974), *3000 Years of Urban Growth* (New York: Academic Press); *World Urbanization Trends*; *State of the World's Cities 2012/13*, 30; Clark, P. (2013), 'Introduction', in Clark (ed.), *Oxford Handbook*, 1–20.

6   *State of the World's Cities 2012/13*, 34–5.

7   *State of the World's Cities 2010/11*; Reeder, D. and Rodger, R. (2000), 'Industrialization and the City Economy', in M. Daunton (ed.), *The Cambridge Urban History of Britain, Volume III: 1840–1950* (Cambridge: Cambridge University Press), 553–92; Hung, H.-F. and Zhan, S. (2013), 'Industrialization and the City: Easy and West', in Clark (ed.), *Oxford Handbook*, 645–63; Bairoch, P. (1988), *Cities and Economic Development from the Dawn of History to the Present* (Chicago: Chicago University Press).

8   Rodger, R. and Sweet, R. (2008), 'The Changing Nature of Urban History', *History in Focus: The City*, at: <www.history.ac.uk/ihr/Focus/City/articles/sweet.html>; Hohenberg, P. and Lees, L. H. (1985), *The Making of Urban Europe 1000–1950* (New Haven: Harvard University Press).

Chapter 1   The Development of Urban History

1   Stave, B. (1979), 'A Conversation with H. J. Dyos: Urban History in Great Britain', *Journal of Urban History* 5: 472.

2   Dyos, H. J. (1968), 'Agenda for Urban Historians', in H. J. Dyos (ed.), *The Study of Urban History* (London: Edward Arnold), 1–46.

3   Jansen, H. (1996), 'Wrestling with the Angel: On Problems of Definition in Urban Historiography', *Urban History* 23: 279; Daunton, M. J. (1978), 'Towns and Economic Growth in Eighteenth Century England', in P. Abrams and E. A. Wrigley, (eds), *Towns in Societies: Essays in Economic History and Historical Sociology* (Cambridge: Cambridge University Press), 276. Braudel is quoted in Rodger, R. (1998), 'In Pursuit of the Indefinable? The Urban Variable Reconsidered', in S. Supphellen (ed.), *The Norwegian Tradition in a European Context* (Trondheim: Trondheim Studies in History), 47–56.

4 Quoted in Cannadine, D. (1982), 'Urban History in the United Kingdom: The "Dyos Phenomenon" and After', in D. Cannadine and D. Reeder (eds), *Exploring the Urban Past: Essays in Urban History by H. J. Dyos* (Cambridge: Cambridge University Press), 209.

5 Hayden, D. (1996), *The Power of Place: Urban Landscapes as Public History* (Cambridge, MA: MIT Press), 15.

6 Reulecke, J., Huck, G. and Sutcliffe, A. (1981), 'Urban History Research in Germany: Its Development and Present Condition', *Urban History Yearbook* 8: 39–41.

7 Pirenne, H. (1925), *Medieval Cities: Their Origins and the Revival of Trade* (Princeton: Princeton University Press).

8 Roche, D. (1980), 'Urban History in France: Achievements, Tendencies and Objectives', *Urban History Yearbook* 7: 12.

9 Lees, A. (1985), *Cities Perceived: Urban Society in European and American Thought, 1820–1940* (Manchester: Manchester University Press), 136–51, 190–3.

10 Gunn, S. (2006), *History and Cultural Theory* (Harlow: Pearson), 107–30.

11 Weber, A. F. (1899), *The Growth of Cities in the Nineteenth Century: A Study in Statistics* (New York: Macmillan), 388.

12 Weber, M. (1958), *The City* (Glencoe: The Free Press). On the Islamic city, see Jayyusi, S. et al. (eds) (2008), *The City in the Islamic World*, 2 vols (Leiden: Brill).

13 Whyte, W. (2014), 'Introduction', in H. Meller (ed.), *Ghent Planning Congress 1913. Premier Congrès International et Exposition Comparée des Villes* (London: Routledge), v–xvii.

14 Hammarström, I. (1978), 'Urban History in Scandinavia', *Urban History Yearbook* 5: 46–55.

15 Gieryn, T. (2006), 'City as Truth-Spot: Laboratories and Field-Sites in Urban Studies', *Social Studies of Science* 36: 6–10.

16 Lampard, E. (1961), 'American Historians and the Study of Urbanization', *American Historical Review* 67: 49–61; Glaab, C. (1965), 'The Historian and the City: A Bibliographic Survey', in P. Hauser and L. Schnore (eds), *The Study of Urbanization* (New York: John Wiley), 53–80; Stave, B. (1974), 'A Conversation with Sam Bass Warner, Jr', *Journal of Urban History* 1: 85–110; Stave, B. (1975), 'A Conversation with Eric E. Lampard', *Journal of Urban History* 1: 440–72.

17 Klemek, C. (2011), *The Transatlantic Collapse of Urban Renewal: Postwar Urbanism from New York to Berlin* (Chicago: University of Chicago Press), 80–1.

18 Jacobs, J. (1961), *The Death and Life of Great American Cities* (New York: Random House); Jacobs, J. (1993), 'Downtown is for People', in W. Whyte, Jr (ed.), *The*

Exploding Metropolis (Berkeley: University of California Press), 160.

19   Gottmann, J. (1961), *Megalopolis: The Urbanized Northeastern Seaboard of the United States* (New York: Twentieth Century Fund).

20   Mumford, L. (1961), *The City in History* (New York: Harcourt Brace).

21   Whyte, Jr, W. (1993), 'Introduction', in Whyte (ed.), *Exploding Metropolis*, 8, 9, 11; Klemek, *Transatlantic Collapse*, 83–101.

22   Handlin, O. (1963), 'The Modern City as a Field of Historical Study', in O. Handlin and J. Burchard (eds), *The Historian and the City* (Cambridge: MIT Press), 1–26.

23   Quoted in Hershberg, T. (1983), 'The Future of Urban History', in D. Fraser and A. Sutcliffe (eds), *The Pursuit of Urban History* (London: Edward Arnold), 429–30.

24   Schnore, L. (ed.) (1975), *The New Urban History: Quantitative Explorations by American Historians* (Princeton: Princeton University Press); Thernstrom, S. and Sennett, R. (eds) (1970), *Nineteenth-century Cities: Essays in the New Urban History* (New Haven: Yale University Press).

25   Stave, 'Conversation with Sam Bass Warner', 92, 100, 108.

26   Reeder, D. (1982), 'Introduction: H. J. Dyos and the Urban Process', in Cannadine and Reeder (eds), *Exploring the Urban Past*, xi.

27   Checkland, S. G., quoted in D. Cannadine (1982), 'Urban History in the United Kingdom: The "Dyos Phenomenon" and After', in Cannadine and Reeder (eds), *Exploring the Urban Past*, 206.

28   Jones, P. (2010), *Unfinished Work: An Essay in Honour of H. J. Dyos 1921–1978* (Leicester: Centre for Urban History); Davies, G. W. (2014), 'The Rise of Urban History in Britain, *c.*1960–1978', unpublished PhD thesis (University of Leicester).

29   Dyos, H. J. (1961), *Victorian Suburb: A Study of the Growth of Camberwell* (Leicester: Leicester University Press), 86.

30   Dyos, 'Agenda for Urban Historians', 7.

31   Dyos, H. J. (1974), 'Editorial', *Urban History Yearbook* 1: 5.

32   Stave, 'Conversation with H. J. Dyos', 493.

33   Checkland, S. G. (1983), 'An Urban History Horoscope', in Fraser and Sutcliffe (eds), *Pursuit of Urban History*, 449–66.

34   Reeder, D. (1998), 'The Industrial City in Britain: Urban Biography in the Modern Style', *Urban History* 25: 368–78; Rodger, R. (2003), 'Taking Stock: Perspectives on British Urban History', *Urban History Review / Revue d'histoire urbaine* 32: 54–63.

35 For a recent example, Madgin, R. and Kenny, N. (eds) (2015), *Comparative and Transnational Approaches to Urban History: Cities beyond Borders* (Aldershot: Ashgate).

36 Checkland, 'Urban History Horoscope', 460–6; Rodger, 'In Pursuit of the Indefinable?'; Hein, C. (2013), 'Port Cities', in Clark (ed.), *Oxford Handbook*, 809–27, quote at 809.

37 Mohl, R. (1974) 'Editorial', *Journal of Urban History* 1: 4; Rodger, R. (1992), 'Urban History: Prospect and Retrospect', *Urban History* 19: 1–22.

38 University of Leicester Dyos Collection: Conferences 3/11, Dyos, H. J. (23 May 1967), 'Some Reflections on the Symposium on the Victorian City, Indiana University, 8–12 March 1967'.

39 Dyos Collection: Correspondence 1/1/1, H. J. Dyos to Derek Aldcroft, 2 December 1973; 1/3/5, S. G. Checkland to Dyos, 26 September 1973; 1/2/9, Peter Burke to Dyos, 12 November 1973.

40 Briggs, A. (1973), 'The Human Aggregate', in H. J. Dyos and M. Wolff (eds), *The Victorian City: Images and Realities*, Volume I (London: Routledge & Kegan Paul), 83.

41 Gilfoyle, T. (2003) 'White Cities, Linguistic Turns, and Disneylands: The New Paradigms of Urban History', *Journal of Urban History* 26: 175–6.

42 Quoted in McShane, C. (2006), 'The State of the Art in North American Urban History', *Journal of Urban History* 32: 588.

43 Gilfoyle, 'White Cities', 180; Domosh, M. (1988), 'The Symbolism of the Skyscraper: Case Studies of New York's First Tall Buildings', *Journal of Urban History* 14: 321–45, quote at 341.

44 Rodger, 'Urban History', 10–12; Doyle, B. M. (2009), 'A Decade of Urban History: Ashgate's Historical Urban Studies Series', *Urban History* 36: 498–512.

45 See here, Stelter, G. and Artibise, A. (eds) (1979), *The Canadian City: Essays in Urban History* (Ottawa: Institute of Canadian Studies); Bickford-Smith, V. (2008), 'Urban History in the New South Africa: Continuity and Innovation since the End of Apartheid', *Urban History* 35: 288–315.

46 Prakash, G. (2002), 'The Urban Turn', in R. Vasudevan et al. (eds), *Sarai Reader 02: Cities of Everyday Life* (Delhi: Centre for the Study of Developing Societies, 2002), 2–7. Population figures are taken from: <http://censusindia.gov.in/>.

47 Prakash, 'Urban Turn', 2.

48 Kidambi, P. (2013), 'Mumbai Modern: Colonial Pasts and Postcolonial Predicaments', *Journal of Urban History* 39: 1003.

49   Gandy, M. (2008), 'Landscapes of Disaster: Water, Modernity, and Urban Fragmentation in Mumbai', *Environment and Planning A* 40: 108–30.
50   Recent examples include Almandoz, A. (ed.) (2002), *Planning Latin America's Capital Cities, 1850–1950* (London: Routledge); Freund, B. (2007), *The African City* (Cambridge: Cambridge University Press); *Urban History* 40 (2013), Special Section on 'Eastern European Cities' edited by M. Prokopovych.; Eldem, E., Goffman, D. and Masters, B. (eds) (1999), *The Ottoman City between East and West: Aleppo, Izmir and Istanbul* (Cambridge: Cambridge University Press); Çelik, Z. (2008), *Empire, Architecture, and the City: French-Ottoman Encounters, 1830–1914* (Seattle: University of Washington Press).
51   Skinner, G. W. (ed.) (1977), *The City in Late Imperial China* (Stanford: Stanford University Press). For more general syntheses of the literature, see Stapleton, K., Shi, M. and McIsaac, M. L. (2000), 'The City in Modern China', *Journal of Urban History* 27: 50; Wasserstrom, J. (2011), 'Introduction', *Urban History* 38: 368; United Nations Department of Economic and Social Affairs (2012), *World Urbanization Prospects: The 2011 Revision* (New York: United Nations).
52   Mitter, R. (2005), *A Bitter Revolution: China's Struggle with the Modern World* (Oxford: Oxford University Press), 42.
53   Rogaski, R. (2004), *Hygienic Modernity: Meanings of Health and Disease in Treaty-Port China* (Berkeley: University of California Press).
54   Henriot, C. (1993), *Shanghai, 1927–1937. Municipal Power, Locality, and Modernization* (Berkeley: University of California Press); Wakeman Jr, F. (1995), *Policing Shanghai, 1927–1937* (Berkeley: University of California Press); Lu, H. (1999), *Beyond the Neon Lights: Everyday Shanghai in the Early Twentieth Century* (Berkeley: University of California Press); Lincoln, T. (2012), 'Revolution in the Streets', *History Today* 62: 44–6.

Chapter 2   Cities, Spaces and Identities

1   Osborne, H. (26 July 2014), 'Poor Doors: The Segregation of Inner-city Flat Dwellers', *Guardian*, at: <http://www.theguardian.com/society/2014/jul/25/poor-doors-segregation-london-flats>; Bellafante, G. (25 July 2014), 'On the Upper West Side, A House Divided by Income', *New York Times*,

at: <http://www.nytimes.com/2014/07/27/nyregion/on-the-upper-west-side-a-house-divided-by-income.html?_r=1>.

2   Recent wide-ranging overviews are provided in Nightingale, C. (2012), *Segregation: A Global History of Divided Cities* (Chicago: University of Chicago Press); Gilbert, A. (2013), 'Poverty, Inequality, and Social Segregation', in Clark (ed.), *World Handbook*, 683–99.

3   Gunn, S. (2001), 'The Spatial Turn: Changing Histories of Space and Place', in S. Gunn and R. J. Morris (eds), *Identities in Space: Contested Terrains in the Western City since 1850* (Aldershot: Ashgate), 5, 9.

4   McCathery, P. (1993), 'Ethnicity and the American City', *Urban History* 20: 78–83.

5   Fischer, B. (2008), *A Poverty of Rights: Citizenship and Inequality in Twentieth-century Rio de Janeiro* (Stanford, California: Stanford University Press), 72.

6   For example, Nicolaides, B. and Wiese, A. (eds) (2006), *The Suburb Reader* (London: Routledge). Jauhiainen, J. (2013), 'Suburbs', in Clark (ed.), *Oxford Handbook of Cities*, 791–808. Excellent overviews of the literature are available in Sies, M. C. (2001), 'North American Suburbs, 1880–1950: Cultural and Social Reconsiderations', *Journal of Urban History* 27: 313–46; McManus, R. and Ethington, P. J. (2007), 'Suburbs in Transition: New Approaches to Suburban History', *Urban History* 34: 317–37.

7   Dyos, *Victorian Suburb*, 22; Warner, S. B. (1962), *Streetcar Suburbs: The Process of Growth in Boston 1870–1900*. (New York: Atheneum).

8   Dyos Collection, 1/23/2, Correspondence, Warner to Dyos, 11 January 1963; Dyos to Warner, 26 February 1963.

9   Warner, *Streetcar Suburbs*, 2–3; Dyos, *Victorian Suburb*, 109–13, quote at 111.

10 Ward, D. (1975), 'Victorian Cities: How Modern?', *Journal of Historical Geography* 1: 135–51; Cannadine, D. (1977), 'Victorian Cities: How Different?', *Social History* 2: 457–87; Sjoberg, G. (1960), *The Pre-Industrial City: Past and Present* (Glencoe: The Free Press); Burke, P. (1976), 'Some Reflections on the Pre-Industrial City', *Urban History Yearbook* 2: 13–21, quote at 16.

11 Jackson, K. T. (1985), *Crabgrass Frontier: The Suburbaniza-tion of the United States* (New York: Oxford University Press), 243–66; Jackson, K. T. (1980), 'Federal Subsidy and the Sub-urban Dream: The First Quarter-Century of Government Inter-vention in the Housing Market', *Records of the Columbia Historical Society* 40: 421–51; Park, R. E., Burgess, E. W., and

McKenzie, R. (1925), *The City* (Chicago: University of Chicago Press).

12 For one excellent microscopic study of this trend, see Beresford, M. W. (1988), *East End, West End: The Face of Leeds during Urbanization, 1684–1842* (Leeds: Thoresby Society).

13 Cannadine, 'Victorian Cities: How Different?', 460–8; Daunton, M. J. (1977), *Coal Metropolis, Cardiff 1870–1914* (Leicester: Leicester University Press).

14 Jackson, *Crabgrass Frontier*, 288–96.

15 Davison, G. (1995), 'Australia: The First Suburban Nation?' *Journal of Urban History* 22: 40–74; quote at 49.

16 Dennis, R. (1984), *English Industrial Cities of the Nineteenth Century: A Social Geography* (Cambridge: Cambridge University Press); Pooley, C. G. (1977), 'The Residential Segregation of Migrant Communities in Mid–Victorian Liverpool', *Transactions of the Institute of British Geographers* 2: 364–82; Lawton, R. (1979), 'Mobility in Nineteenth Century British Cities', *Geographical Journal* 145: 206–24; Lilley, K. (2000), 'Mapping the Medieval City: Plan Analysis and Urban History', *Urban History* 27: 5–30; Scobie, J. (1974), *Buenos Aires: Plaza to Suburb, 1870–1910* (New York: Oxford University Press); Almandoz (ed.), *Planning Latin America's Capital Cities*; Urban, F. (2011), *Tower and Slab: Histories of Global Mass Housing* (London: Routledge).

17 Harris, R. and Lewis, R. (2001), 'The Geography of North American Cities and Suburbs, 1900–1950: A New Synthesis', *Journal of Urban History* 27: 262–92; quote at 272; Harris, R. (1996), *Unplanned Suburbs: Toronto's American Tragedy, 1900 to 1950* (Baltimore: The Johns Hopkins University Press), chs. 2–3; Zunz, O. (2000), *The Changing Face of Inequality: Urbanization, Industrial Development and Immigrants in Detroit, 1880–1920* (Chicago: Chicago University Press), 354–9; Wiese, A. (2004), *Places of Their Own: African American Suburbanization in the Twentieth Century* (Chicago: Chicago University Press).

18 Flanagan, M. (1997), 'Women in the City, Women of the City: Where do Women Fit in Urban History?', *Journal of Urban History* 23: 251–9; Gunn, S. (2004), 'Class, Identity and the Urban: The Middle Class in England, c.1790–1950', *Urban History* 31: 35–8.

19 Hall, C. and Davidoff, L. (1983), 'The Architecture of Public and Private Life: English Middle-Class Society in a Provincial Town 1780 to 1850', in Fraser and Sutcliffe (eds), *Pursuit of Urban History*, 326–45.

20 Miller, R. (1983), 'The Hoover in the Garden: Middle Class Women and Suburbanization, 1850–1920', *Environment and Planning D: Society and Space* 1: 73–87; Marsh, M. (1990), *Suburban Lives* (New Brunswick: Rutgers University Press); Strong-Boag, V., Dyck, I., England, K., and Johnson, L. (1999), 'What Women's Spaces? Women in Australian, British, Canadian and US Suburbs', in R. Harris and P. J. Larkham (eds), *Changing Suburbs: Foundation, Form and Function* (London: E. & F.N. Spon), 168–86.

21 Flanagan, M. (1966), 'The City Livable: Environmental Policy, Gender, and Power in Chicago in the 1910s', *Journal of Urban History* 22: 164; Meller, (1990), 'Planning Theory and Women's Role in the City', *Urban History Yearbook* 17: 86.

22 Jackson, *Crabgrass Frontier*, 234–8.

23 Kelly, B. (1993), *Expanding the American Dream: Building and Rebuilding Levittown* (Albany: State University of New York Press).

24 Strong-Boag et al., 'What Women's Spaces?', 177.

25 For example, Chauncey, G. (1994), *Gay New York: Gender, Urban Culture, and the Makings of the Gay Male World, 1890–1940* (New York: Basic Books); Armstrong, E. (2002), *Forging Gay Identities: Organizing Sexuality in San Francisco, 1950–1994* (Chicago: University of Chicago Press).

26 Hodge, S. (1995), '"No Fags Out There": Gay Men, Identity and Suburbia', *Journal of Interdisciplinary Gender Studies* 1: 41–8.

27 Gooptu, N. (2001), *The Politics of the Urban Poor in Early Twentieth-Century India* (Cambridge: Cambridge University Press), quote at 7. See also Jones, G. S. (1976), *Outcast London: A Study in the Relationship Between Classes in Victorian Society* (Harmondsworth: Penguin); Chandavarkar, R. (1994), *The Origins of Industrial Capitalism in India: Business Strategies and the Working Classes in Bombay, 1900–1940* (Cambridge: Cambridge University Press); Ferguson, J. (1999), *Expectations of Modernity: Myths and Meanings of Urban Life on the Zambian Copperbelt* (Berkeley: University of California Press).

28 Morris, R. J. (2000), 'The Industrial Town', in P. J. Waller (ed.), *The English Urban Landscape* (Oxford: Oxford University Press), 175–208.

29 Dyos, H. J. (1982), 'The Slums of Victorian London', in Cannadine and Reeder (eds), *Exploring the Urban Past*, 129–53; Dyos, H. J. and Reeder, D. (1973), 'Slums and Suburbs', in Dyos and Wolff (eds), *Victorian City*, 363; Rodger, R. (2000),

'Slums and Suburbs: The Persistence of Residential Apartheid', in Waller (ed.), *English Urban Landscape*, 233–68.

30　Mayne, A. (1990), 'Representing the Slum', *Urban History Yearbook* 17, quote at 69; Mayne, A. (1993), *The Imagined Slum: Newspaper Representation in Three Cities 1870–1914* (Leicester: Leicester University Press), quote at 129.

31　See da Silva Pereira, M. (2002), 'The Time of the Capitals: Rio de Janeiro and São Paulo: Words, Actors and Plans', in Almandoz (ed.), *Planning Latin America's Capital Cities*, 75–108; Freund, B. (2013), 'Africa: 1000–2010', in Clark (ed.), *Oxford Handbook*, 634–5.

32　Lu, H. (1995), 'Creating Urban Outcasts: Shantytowns in Shanghai, 1920–1950', *Journal of Urban History* 21: 563–96, quote at 580.

33　Olsen, D. (1988), *The City as a Work of Art: London, Paris, Vienna* (New Haven: Yale University Press); Maderthaner, W. and Musner, L. (2008), *Unruly Masses: The Other Side of Fin-de-Siècle Vienna* (Oxford: Berghahn Books).

34　Davis, M. (2007), *Planet of Slums* (London: Verso), 54–5, 103–7; Shin, H. B. and Li, B. (2012), *Migrants, Landlords and Their Uneven Experiences of the Beijing Olympic Games* (London: London School of Economics' Centre for Analysis of Social Exclusion).

35　Platt, H. (2010), 'Exploding Cities: Housing the Masses in Paris, Chicago, and Mexico City, 1850–2000', *Journal of Urban History* 36: 575–80.

36　Platt, 'Exploding Cities', 575–83; quotes at 581 and 583; Zunz, *Changing Face of Inequality*, 375–8; Nightingale, *Segregation*, ch.10.

37　Freund, *African City*, 78–82, 148–9; Bickford-Smith, V. (1995), *Ethnic Pride and Racial Prejudice in Victorian Cape Town* (Cambridge: Cambridge University Press), 25, 67–90.

38　Kidambi, P. (2001) 'Housing the Poor in a Colonial City: The Bombay Improvement Trust, 1898–1918', *Studies in History* 17: 57–79; Gooptu, *Politics of the Urban Poor*, 66.

39　Gooptu, *Politics of the Urban Poor*, 14.

40　Gooptu, *Politics of the Urban Poor*, 93–101, quote at 101; Fischer, *Poverty of Rights*, 36–7.

41　Davis, *Planet of Slums*, 140–2.

42　Biswas, S. (30 May 2014) 'Why India's Sanitation Crisis Kills Women', BBC News Online, at: <http://www.bbc.co.uk/news/world-asia-india-27635363>.

43　Mayne, 'Representing the Slum', 77–8.

44　Fischer, *Poverty of Rights*, 54–6, 71–81, quote at 80.

45　Fischer, *Poverty of Rights*, 65–8, quote at 68.

Chapter 3   Governing Cities

1   Edouard Herriot, mayor of Lyon, quoted in Cohen, W. (1998) *Urban Government and the Rise of the French City: Five Municipalities in the Nineteenth Century* (Basingstoke: Macmillan), xii.

2   Dagenais, M., Maver, I., and Saunier, P.-Y. (eds), *Municipal Services and Employees in the Modern City: New Historic Approaches* (Aldershot: Ashgate); Garrard, J. (ed.), *Heads of the Local State: Mayors, Provosts and Burgomasters since 1800* (Aldershot: Ashgate); Soffer, J. (2010), *Ed Koch and the Rebuilding of New York City* (New York: Columbia University Press), 9–10.

3   Evelyn Sharp, cited in Hennock, E. P. (1967), 'The Social Composition of Borough Councils in Two Large Cities, 1835–1914', in Dyos (ed.), *Study of Urban History*, 316.

4   Hennock, E. P. (1973), *Fit and Proper Persons: Ideal and Reality in Nineteenth-century Urban Government* (London: Edward Arnold).

5   Hennock, *Fit and Proper Persons*, 170–2; Fraser, D. (1979), *Power and Authority in Victorian England* (Oxford: Blackwell); Sweet, R. (1999), *The English Town, 1680–1840: Government, Society and Culture* (London: Pearson).

6   Hennock, *Fit and Proper Persons*, 361–8; Hennock, 'Social Compositions', 319. Paul Laxton offers a useful synthesis of Hennock's research in Laxton, P. (2013), 'E. P. Hennock: An Appreciation', *Urban History* 40: 726–9.

7   Crossick, G. and Haupt, H–G. (1995), *The Petite Bourgeoisie in Europe 1780–1914: Enterprise, Family and Independence* (London: Routledge); Doyle, B. M. (2007), 'Rehabilitating the Retailer: Shopkeepers in Urban Government, 1900–1950', in S. Couperus, C. Smit and D. J. Wolffram (eds), *In Control of the City: Local Elites and the Dynamics of Urban Politics, 1800–1960* (Leuven: Peeters), 41–52.

8   Garrard, J. (1983), *Leadership and Power in Victorian Industrial Towns 1830–80* (Manchester: Manchester University Press); Trainor, R. H. (1993), *Black Country Elites: The Exercise of Authority in an Industrial Area 1830–1900* (Oxford: Oxford University Press); Doyle, B. M. (1997), 'The Structure of Elite Power in the Early Twentieth-century City: Norwich, 1900–35', *Urban History* 24: 179–99.

9   Miskell, L. (2007), 'Urban Power, Industrialization and Political Reform: Swansea Elites in the Town and Region, 1780–1850', in R. Roth and R. Beachy (eds), *Who Ran the Cities?*

City Elites and Urban Power Structures in Europe and North America, 1750–1940 (Aldershot: Ashgate), 21–36; Corfield, P. (1982), *The Impact of English Towns* (Oxford: Oxford University Press), 177–8; Sweet, *English Town*, 147.

10   Ewen, S. (2004), 'Power and Administration in Two Midland Cities, *c.*1870–1938', unpublished PhD thesis (University of Leicester); Hennock, 'Social Composition', 324; Moore, J. and Rodger, R. (2007), 'Who Really Ran the Cities? Municipal Knowledge and Policy Networks in British Local Government, 1832–1914', in Roth and Beachy (eds), *Who Ran The Cities?*, 51.

11   Hayes, N. (1996), *Consensus and Controversy: City Politics in Nottingham 1945–1966* (Liverpool: Liverpool University Press); Doyle, 'Structure of Elite Power', 179–99.

12   Kaal, H. (2007), 'Key to the City: New Elites in Amsterdam and Mayor Willem de Vlugt, 1921–1941', in Couperus, Smit and Wolffram (eds), *In Control of the City*, 53–68; Couperus, S. (2007), 'Backstage Politics: Municipal Directors and Technocratic Ambitions in Amsterdam, 1916–1930', in Couperus, Smit and Wolffram (eds), *In Control of the City*, 175–89.

13   Hanes, J. (2002), *The City as Subject: Seki Hajime and the Reinvention of Modern Osaka* (Berkeley: University of California Press); Lafi, N. (2005), *Municipalités Méditerranéennes. Les Réformes Urbaines Ottomanes au Miroir d'une Histoire Comparée* (Berlin: Klaus Schwarz Verlag).

14   Henriot, *Shanghai, 1927–1937*.

15   Geertz, C. (1973), *The Interpretation of Cultures: Selected Essays* (New York: Basic Books).

16   Morris, R. J. (2000), 'Governance: Two Centuries of Urban Growth', in R. J. Morris and R. H. Trainor (eds), *Urban Governance: Britain and Beyond since 1750.* (Aldershot: Ashgate), 1.

17   Roth, R. (2007), 'German Urban Elites in the Eighteenth and Nineteenth Centuries', in Roth and Beachy (eds), *Who Ran The Cities?*, 127–60.

18   Morris, R. J. (1983), 'Voluntary Societies and British Urban Elites, 1780–1850: An Analysis', *Historical Journal* 26: 95–118; Morris, R. J. (1990), *Class, Sect and Party: The Making of the British Middle Class* (Manchester: Manchester University Press); Morris, R. J. (1998), 'Civil Society and the Nature of Urbanism: Britain, 1750–1850', *Urban History* 25: 291; Roth, 'German Urban Elites', 148.

19   Valérian, D. (2013), 'Middle East: 7th–15th Centuries', in Clark (ed.), *Oxford Handbook*, 258–74; Boyar, E. (2013),

'The Ottoman City: 1500–1800, in Clark (ed.), *Oxford Handbook*, 275–91, quote at 285.

20 Morris, 'Governance', 1.

21 Morris, 'Civil Society', 296–7; Morton, G., de Vries, B., and Morris, R. J. (eds), (2006) *Civil Society, Associations and Urban Places: Class, Nation and Culture in Nineteenth-Century Europe* (Aldershot: Ashgate).

22 Rodger, R. (2001), *The Transformation of Edinburgh: Land, Property and Trust in the Nineteenth Century* (Cambridge: Cambridge University Press).

23 DiGaetano, A. (2009), 'The Birth of Modern Urban Governance: A Comparison of Political Modernization in Boston, Massachusetts, and Bristol, England, 1880–1870', *Journal of Urban History* 35: 259–87.

24 DiGaetano, 'Modern Urban Governance', quote at 262.

25 DiGaetano, 'Modern Urban Governance', 267–79; Prest, J. (1990), *Liberty and Locality: Parliament, Permissive Legislation, and Ratepayers' Democracies in the Nineteenth Century* (Oxford: Clarendon Press); Miller, Z. (1970), *Boss Cox's Cincinnati: Urban Politics in the Progressive Era* (New York: Oxford University Press); Flanagan, M. (2006), *America Reformed: Progressives and Progressivism, 1890s–1920s* (New York: Oxford University Press).

26 Gordon, C., Miller, P. and Burchell, G. (eds) (1991), *The Foucault Effect: Studies in Governmentality* (Hemel Hempstead: Harvester Wheatsheaf).

27 Joyce, P. (2003), *The Rule of Freedom: Liberalism and the Modern City* (London: Verso).

28 Otter, C. (2008), *The Victorian Eye: A Political History of Light and Vision in Britain, 1800–1910* (Chicago: University of Chicago Press); Croll, A. (2000), *Civilizing the Urban: Popular Culture and Public Space in Merthyr, c.1870–1914* (Cardiff: University of Wales Press).

29 Falkus, M. (1969), 'The British Gas Industry before 1850', *Economic History Review*, Second Series 20: 494–508.

30 Ewen, 'Power and Administration', 232–6.

31 Joyce and Otter both use Bruno Latour's phrase 'black boxing' to refer to the ways in which sanitation and lighting reforms were treated as matters of science and technology, and divorced from the political apparatus: Latour, B. (1987), *Science in Action: How to Follow Scientists and Engineers through Society* (Cambridge, MA: Harvard University Press).

32 For examples, Brown-May, A. (1998), *Melbourne Street Life: The Itinerary of Our Days* (Kew, Victoria: Australian Scholarly); Furnée, J.-H. (2013), '"Le bon public de la Haye". Local

Governance and the Audience in the French Opera in The Hague, 1820–1890', *Urban History* 40: 624–45; Kenny, N. (2014), *The Feel of the City: Experiences of Urban Transformation* (Toronto: University of Toronto Press).

Chapter 4 Cities and the Environment

1 McNeill, J. (2000), *Something New Under the Sun: An Environmental History of the Twentieth-Century World* (York: W.W. Norton), 282, 353–4.

2 Tarr, J. A. (1996), *The Search for the Ultimate Sink: Urban Pollution in Historical Perspective* (Akron: University of Akron Press), xxix.

3 Melosi, M. V. (2010), 'Humans, Cities, and Nature: How Do Cities Fit in the Material World?', *Journal of Urban History* 36: 4.

4 Mosley, S. (2006), 'Common Ground: Integrating Social and Environmental History', *Journal of Social History* 39: 915–33; Gunn, S. and Owens, A. (2006), 'Nature, Technology and the Modern City: An Introduction', *Cultural Geographies* 13: 494.

5 Melosi, M. (2011), 'Mainstreaming Environmental History', and Walker, R., 'On the Edge of Environmental History', in K. Coulter and C. Mauch (eds), *The Future of Environmental History: Needs and Opportunities* (Munich: Rachel Carson Center for Environment and Society), 33, 48–52.

6 Worster, D. (1988), *The Ends of the Earth: Perspectives on Modern Environmental History* (Cambridge: Cambridge University Press), 292.

7 Worster, D. (1990), 'Transformations of the Earth: Toward an Agroecological Perspective in History', *Journal of American History* 76: 1088–9.

8 Worster, *Ends of the Earth*, 8–10. On the historical value of the anthropocene, Chakrabarty, D. (2009), 'The Climate of History: Four Theses', *Critical Enquiry* 35: 207–8.

9 Worster, 'Transformations of the Earth', 1090–1.

10 Worster, *Ends of the Earth*, 292–3.

11 Cronon, W. (1990), 'Modes of Prophecy and Production: Placing Nature in History', *Journal of American History* 76: 1130.

12 Melosi, 'Humans, Cities, and Nature', 5, 8, 14; Jacobs, *Death and Life*, 443–4.

13 Rosen, C. M. and Tarr, J. A. (1994), 'The Importance of an Urban Perspective in Environmental History', *Journal of Urban History* 20: 307.

14 Cronon, W. (1991), *Nature's Metropolis: Chicago and the Great West* (New York: W.W. Norton).

15 Sawislak, K. (1995), *Smoldering City: Chicagoans and the Great Fire, 1871–1874* (Chicago: Chicago University Press); Smith, C. (1995), *Urban Disorder and the Shape of Belief: The Great Chicago Fire, the Haymarket Bomb, and the Model Town of Pullman* (Chicago: University of Chicago Press).

16 Sawislak, *Smoldering City*, ch. 2; Rosen, C. M. (1986), *The Limits of Power: Great Fires and the Process of City Growth in America* (Cambridge: Cambridge University Press).

17 Wermiel, S. (2000), *The Fireproof Building: Technology and Public Safety in the Nineteenth-Century American City* (Baltimore: The Johns Hopkins University Press), 81.

18 The City Museum offers regular and permanent exhibitions of the fire. See the Chicago History Museum's Website for more details: <http://chicagohistory.org/>. Alternatively, online exhibitions and tours are available via The Great Chicago Fire & The Web of Memory at: <http://www.greatchicagofire.org/>. Recent documentary films include *Chicago: City of the Century* (PBS, 2003) and an episode of *Unsolved History*, 'Great Chicago Fire', season 2, episode 10 (10 February 2004).

19 Good early examples include Hamlin, C. (1988), 'Muddling in Bumbledom: On the Enormity of Large Sanitary Improvements in Four British Towns, 1855–1885', *Victorian Studies* 32: 55–83; Tarr, *Ultimate Sink*; Melosi, M. V. (1999), *The Sanitary City: Urban Infrastructure in America from Colonial Times to the Present* (Baltimore: The Johns Hopkins University Press).

20 Bernhardt, C. (ed.) (2001), *Environmental Problems in European Cities in the 19th and 20th Century* (Münster: Waxmann); Schott, D., Luckin, B. and Massard-Guilbard, G. (eds) (2005), *Resources of the City: Contributions to an Environmental History of Modern Europe* (Aldershot: Ashgate); Mosley, S. and Massard-Guilbaud, G. (eds) (2011), *Common Ground: Integrating the Social and Environmental in History* (Newcastle: Cambridge Scholars Publishing).

21 Platt, H. L. (2005) *Shock Cities: The Environmental Transformation and Reform of Manchester and Chicago* (Chicago: Chicago University Press), quote at xiv.

22 For example, Wohl, A. S. (1983), *Endangered Lives: Public Health in Victorian Britain* (London: J. M. Dent & Sons); Luckin, B. (1986), *Pollution and Control: A Social History of the Thames in the Nineteenth Century* (Bristol: Hilger); Bernhardt, C. and Massard-Guilbaud, G. (eds) (2002), *The Modern Demon: Pollution in Urban and Industrial European Societies* (Clermont-Ferrand: Presses Universitaires Blaise-Pascal);

Thompson, F. M. L. (1976), 'Nineteenth-Century Horse Sense', *The Economic History Review*, New Series 29: 60–81; McShane, C. and Tarr, J. A. (2007), *The Horse in the City: Living Machines in the Nineteenth Century* (Baltimore: The Johns Hopkins University Press).

23   For a flavour of the increasing variety of urban histories of water, Pinol, J.-L. and Menjot, D. (eds) (2000), *Water and European Cities from the Middle Ages to the Nineteenth Century* (Aldershot: Ashgate); Blackbourn, D. (2007), *The Conquest of Nature: Water, Landscape and the Making of Modern Germany* (New York: W.W. Norton); Brioch, J. (2013), *London: Water and the Making of the Modern City* (Pittsburgh: University of Pittsburgh Press); Smith, C. (2013), *City Water, City Life: Water and the Infrastructure of Ideas in Urbanizing Philadelphia, Boston, and Chicago* (Chicago: University of Chicago Press); Guillerme, A. (2013), *The Age of Water: The Urban Environment in the North of France, A.D. 300–1800* (Austin: Texas A&M University Press).

24   One such recent comparative study is Gotham, K. F. and Greenberg, M. (2014) *Crisis Cities: Disaster and Redevelopment in New York and New Orleans* (New York: Oxford University Press).

25   Ewen, S. (2014), 'Sheffield's Great Flood of 1864: Engineering Failure and the Municipalisation of Water', *Environment & History* 20: 177–207; Ewen, S. (2014), 'Socio-technological Disasters and Engineering Expertise in Victorian Britain: The Holmfirth and Sheffield Floods of 1852 and 1864', *Journal of Historical Geography* 46: 13–25.

26   Weintritt, O. (2009), 'The Floods of Baghdad: Cultural and Technological Responses', in C. Mauch and C. Pfister (eds) (2009), *Natural Disasters, Cultural Responses: Case Studies Toward a Global Environmental History* (Lanham: Lexington Books), 165–82.

27   Tarr, *Ultimate Sink*, 8–9.

28   Smith, *City Water*, 14–27.

29   Smith, *City Water*, 5, 52.

30   Philo, C. (2000), 'More Words, More Worlds: Reflections on the "Cultural Turn" and Human Geography', in I. Cook, D. Crouch, S. Naylor and J. Ryan (eds) (2000), *Cultural Turns / Geographical Turns: Perspectives on Cultural Geography* (Harlow: Prentice Hall), 33.

31   Swyngedouw, E. (2004), *Social Power and the Urbanization of Water: Flows of Power* (Oxford: Oxford University Press); Gandy, M. (2002), *Concrete and Clay: Reworking Nature in New York City* (Cambridge, MA: MIT Press); Kaika, M.

(2005), *City of Flows: Modernity, Nature, and the City* (London: Routledge); Falck, Z. (2011), *Weeds: An Environmental History of Metropolitan America* (Pittsburgh: University of Pittsburgh Press).

32 Gandy, *Concrete and Clay*, 22–3.

33 Gandy, *Concrete and Clay*, 32, 35.

34 Gandy, *Concrete and Clay*, 19, 28–9.

35 Frioux, S. (2012), 'At a Green Crossroads: Recent Theses in Urban Environmental History in Europe and North America', *Urban History* 39: 529, 538–9; Glaeser, E. (2011), *Triumph of the City: How Urban Spaces Make Us Human* (London: Macmillan); Hall, P. (2013), *Good Cities, Better Lives: How Europe Discovered the Lost Art of Urbanism* (London: Routledge).

36 For recent examples, Elvin, M. (2004), *The Retreat of the Elephants: An Environmental History of China* (New Haven: Yale University Press); Mikhail, A. (2012), *Nature and Empire in Ottoman Egypt: An Environmental History* (Cambridge: Cambridge University Press); Mikhail, A. (ed.) (2013), *Water on Sand: Environmental Histories of the Middle East and North Africa* (Oxford: Oxford University Press); Josephson, P. et al. (2013), *An Environmental History of Russia* (Cambridge: Cambridge University Press).

37 Mauch, C. (2009) 'Introduction', in Mauch and Pfister (eds), *Natural Disasters, Cultural Responses*, 9.

38 Bankoff, G. (2012), 'A Tale of Two Cities: The Pyro-Seismic Morphology of Nineteenth-Century Manila', in G. Bankoff, U. Lübken and J. Sand (eds), *Flammable Cities: Urban Conflagration and the Making of the Modern World* (Madison: University of Wisconsin Press), 170–89; Bankoff, G. (2009), 'Cultures of Disaster, Cultures of Coping: Hazard as a Frequent Life Experience in the Philippines', in Mauch and Pfister (eds), *Natural Disasters, Cultural Responses*, 265–84; Frost, L. (1997), 'Coping in Their Own Way: Asian Cities and the Problem of Fires', *Urban History* 24: 5–16.

39 Mauch, 'Introduction', 9.

40 Davies, A. R. (2012), 'Points of Origin: The Social Impact of the 1906 San Francisco Earthquake and Fire', in Bankoff, Lübken and Sands (eds), *Flammable Cities*, 273–92; Ewen, S. (2010), *Fighting Fires: Creating the British Fire Service, 1800–1978* (Basingstoke: Palgrave), 30–50; Massard-Guilbaud, G. and Rodger, R. (eds) (2011), *Environmental and Social Justice in the City: Historical Perspectives* (Cambridge: White Horse Press).

41 Wilson, G. (2009), 'The City and Public History', *Journal of Urban History* 20: 1–12.

Chapter 5   Urban Culture and Modernity

1   Wirth, L. (1938), 'Urbanism as a Way of Life', *American Journal of Sociology* 44: 1–24.

2   De Certeau, M. (1984), *The Practice of Everyday Life* (Berkeley: University of California Press).

3   A good example of this literature is Esherick, J. (ed.) (2000), *Remaking the Chinese City: Modernity and National Identity, 1900–1950* (Honolulu: University of Hawai'i Press).

4   Berman, M. (1983), *All That is Solid Melts into Air: The Experience of Modernity* (London: Verso), 15.

5   See the introduction to Rieger, B. and Daunton, M. J. (eds) (2001), *Meanings of Modernity: Britain from the Late-Victorian Era to World War II* (Oxford: Berg).

6   Gunn, *History and Cultural Theory*, 122–3.

7   Olsen, *City as a Work of Art*, 35–53, 69–81; quotes at 43, 69, 73.

8   Gunn, S. (2000), *The Public Culture of the Victorian Middle Class: Ritual and Authority in the English Industrial City 1840–1914* (Manchester: Manchester University Press), 36–59, quotes at 37, 41.

9   Almandoz, A. (2002), 'Urbanization and Urbanism in Latin America: From Haussmann to CIAM', in Almandoz (ed.), *Planning Latin America's Capital Cities*, 13–44, quote at 24.

10 Volait, M. and Al-Asad, M. (2013), 'Middle East', in Clark (ed.), *Oxford Handbook*, 604–11; Hanssen, J. (2005), *Fin de Siècle Beirut: The Making of an Ottoman Provincial Capital* (Oxford: Oxford University Press); Çelik, Z. (2008), *Empire, Architecture, and the City: French–Ottoman Encounters, 1830–1914* (Seattle: University of Washington Press); Elsheshtawy, Y. (ed.) (2008), *The Evolving Arab City: Tradition, Modernity and Urban Development* (New York: Routledge); Elsheshtawy, Y. (ed.) (2009), *Planning Middle Eastern Cities: An Urban Kaleidoscope* (New York: Routledge); Gül, M. (2009), *The Emergence of Modern Istanbul: Transformation and Modernisation of a City* (London: Tauris); Kassir, S. (2010), *Beirut* (Berkeley: University of California Press).

11 Steinberg, M. (2011), *Petersburg Fin de Siècle* (New Haven: Yale University Press), 10–17, 63–5, quotes at 63 and 11.

12 Steinberg, *Petersburg*, 63; Gunn, *Public Culture*, 60–1.

13 Schorske, C. (1980), *Fin-de-siècle Vienna: Politics and Culture* (New York: Knopf); Bender, T. and Schorske, C. (1994), *Budapest and New York: Studies in Metropolitan Transformation, 1870–1930* (New York: Russell Sage); Gyani, G. (2004),

Identity and the Urban Experience: Fin-de-Siècle Budapest. (Wayne, New Jersey: Center for Hungarian Studies and Publications).

14 Gimbel, B. (12 March 2007), 'The Richest City in the World', *Fortune*, at: <http://archive.fortune.com/magazines/fortune/fortune_archive/2007/03/19/8402357/index.htm>; Chatterton, P. and Hodkinson, S. (spring 2007), 'Leeds: Skyscraper City', *The Yorkshire and Humber Regional Review*, 30–2.

15 Ladd, B. (1997), *The Ghosts of Berlin: Confronting German History in the Urban Landscape* (Chicago: University of Chicago Press), 175–216; Goldberger, P. (2001), 'The World Trade Center: Rising in Sheer Exaltation', in S. Costello (ed.), *The World Trade Center Remembered* (New York: Abbeville Press), 14. See also Goldberger, P. (1986), *The Skyscraper* (New York: Knopf); Nasr, J. (2003), 'Planning Histories, Urban Futures, and the World Trade Center Attack', *Journal of Planning History* 2: 195–211; Page, M. (2008), *The City's End: Two Centuries of Fantasies, Fears, and Premonitions of New York's Destruction* (New Haven: Yale University Press), 189–203.

16 Isenberg, A. (2004), *Downtown America: A History of the Place and the People Who Made It* (Chicago: University of Chicago Press), 4–5, 50–8.

17 Walkowitz, J. (1992), *City of Dreadful Delight: Narratives of Sexual Danger in Late-Victorian London* (London: Virago), quote at 46; Nead, L. (2000), *Victorian Babylon: People, Streets, and Images in Nineteenth-century London* (New Haven: Yale University Press); Rappaport, E. (2000), *Shopping for Pleasure: Women in the Making of London's West End* (Princeton: Princeton University Press).

18 Rappaport, E. (1996), '"The Halls of Temptation": Gender, Politics, and the Construction of the Department Store in Late Victorian London', *Journal of British Studies* 35: 58–83; Brown-May, *Melbourne Street Life*, 95–107; quote at 106.

19 Volait and Al-Asad, 'Middle East', 611.

20 Simon, B. (2002), 'New York Avenue: The Life and Death of Gay Spaces in Atlantic City, New Jersey, 1920–1990', *Journal of Urban History* 28: 300–27, quote at 314.

21 Simon, 'New York Avenue', 319–21.

22 Fishman, R. (1982), *Urban Utopias in the Twentieth Century: Ebenezer Howard, Frank Lloyd Wright, Le Corbusier* (Cambridge, MA: MIT Press).

23 McShane, C. (1999), 'The Origins and Globalization of Traffic Control Signals', *Journal of Urban History* 25:

379–404; Gunn, S. (2010), 'The Rise and Fall of British Urban Modernism: Planning Bradford 1945–1970', *Journal of British Studies* 58: 849–69; Biles, R., Mohl, R. and Rose, M. (2014), 'Revisiting the Urban Interstates: Politics, Policy, and Culture since World War II', *Journal of Urban History* 40: 827–30.

24 Klemek, *Transatlantic Collapse of Urban Renewal*, 21–77; Shoshkes, E. (2013), *Jaqueline Tyrwhitt: A Transnational Life in Urban Planning and Design* (Aldershot: Ashgate).

25 Jacobs, 'Downtown is for People', quotes at 160, 165.

26 Hollow, M. (2010), 'Governmentality on the Park Hill Estate: The Rationality of Public Housing', *Urban History* 37: 127; Moran, J. (2012), 'Imagining the Street in Post–War Britain', *Urban History* 39: 166–86.

27 Moran, 'Imagining the Street', 175–7; Shapely, P. (2011), 'Planning, Housing and Participation in Britain, 1968–1976', *Planning Perspectives* 26: 75–90.

28 Calavita, N. and Ferrer, A. (2000), 'Behind Barcelona's Success Story: Citizen Movements and Planners' Power', *Journal of Urban History* 26: 793–807; Mohl, R. (2004), 'Stop the Road: Freeway Revolts in American Cities', *Journal of Urban History* 30: 674–706; Klemek, *Transatlantic Collapse*, 133–60; Haumann, S. (2013), 'Disputed Transformations: Deindustrialization and Redevelopment of Cologne's "Stollwerck" Factory, 1970–1980', *Urban History* 40: 156–73.

29 Fischer, *Poverty of Rights*, 62–6; Lu, 'Creating Urban Outcasts', 573.

30 Chopra, P. (2011), *A Joint Enterprise: Indian Elites and the Making of British Bombay* (Minneapolis: University of Minnesota Press), 73–115, quotes at 78 and 114; Chattopadhyay, S. (2005), *Representing Calcutta: Modernity, Nationalism, and the Colonial Uncanny* (London: Routledge); Abu-Lughod, J. (1980), *Rabat: Urban Apartheid in Morocco* (Princeton: Princeton University Press); Bickford-Smith, *Ethnic Pride and Racial Prejudice*.

31 Volait and Al-Asad, 'Middle East', 609; Dong, M. Y. (2000), 'Defining Beiping: Urban Reconstruction and National Identity, 1928–1936', in Esherick (ed.), *Remaking the Chinese City*, 121–35.

32 Gyani, *Identity and the Urban Experience*.

33 Gunn, *History and Cultural Theory*, 124–6.

34 Steinberg, *Petersburg*, 24–6; Walkowitz, *City of Dreadful Delight*, 15–18.

35 Fritzsche, P. (1996), *Reading Berlin 1900* (Cambridge, MA: Harvard University Press), 4–9; Steinberg, *Petersburg*, 58.

36 *Man With A Movie Camera*, dir. Dziga Vertov (1929).

37 *Man With A Movie Camera*; Walkowitz, *City of Dreadful Delight*, 41–80.
38 Chauncey, *Gay New York*, 179–206.
39 Churchill, D. (2004), 'Mother Goose's Map: Tabloid Geographies and Gay Male Experience in 1950s Toronto', *Journal of Urban History* 30: 837–8; Houlbrook, M. (2005), *Queer London: Perils and Pleasures in the Sexual Metropolis, 1918–1957* (Chicago: Chicago University Press), 1–8, 264–5, quote at 4; Chauncey, *Gay New York*, 179.
40 Houlbrook, *Queer London*, 5, 222–3; Churchill, 'Mother Goose's Map', 827–8.

Chapter 6   Transnational Urban History

1   Quoted in Vertovec, S. (2009), *Transnationalism* (London: Routledge), 10.
2   Appadurai, A. (1996), *Modernity at Large: Cultural Dimensions of Globalization* (Minneapolis: University of Minnesota Press).
3   Smith, M. P. (2001), *Transnational Urbanism: Locating Globalization* (Oxford: Blackwell).
4   Sellers, J. (2005), 'Re-placing the Nation: An Agenda for Comparative Urban Politics', *Urban Affairs Review* 60: 420.
5   Hall, P. (1998), *Cities in Civilization: Culture, Innovation and Urban Order.* (London: Weidenfeld); Hietala, M. and Clark, P. (2013), 'Creative Cities', in Clark (ed.), *Oxford Handbook*, 720–36.
6   Warner, S. B., Jr (1972), *The Urban Wilderness: A History of the American City* (New York: Harper & Row), 57.
7   Saunier, P.-Y. (2008), 'Learning by Doing: Notes about the Making of the Palgrave Dictionary of Transnational History', *Journal of Modern European History* 6: 159–80.
8   Iriye, A. and Saunier, P.-Y. (2009), 'Introduction: The Professor and the Madman', in A. Iriye and P.-Y. Saunier (eds), *The Palgrave Dictionary of Transnational History* (New York: Palgrave), xviii.
9   Seigel, M. (2005), 'Beyond Compare: Comparative Method after the Transnational Turn', *Radical History Review* 9: 63.
10 Bayly, C. A., Beckert, S., Connelly, M., Hofmeyr, I., Kozol, W. and Seed, P. (2006), 'AHR Conversation: On Transnational History', *American Historical Review* 111: 1442–3.
11 'AHR Conversation', comments from Beckert, 1445.

12   Examples include: Saunier, P.-Y. (ed.) (2002), 'Special Issue: Municipal Connections: Co-operation, Links and Transfers among European Cities in the Twentieth Century', *Contemporary European History* 11: 507–640; Ethington, P., Reiff, J. and Levitus, D. (eds) (2009), 'Special Issue: Transnational Urbanism in the Americas', *Urban History* 36: 195–326. Palgrave Macmillan has a Transnational History Series, edited by Akira Iriye and Rana Mitter.

13   Examples of this literature include: Sutcliffe, A. S. (1981), *Towards the Planned City: Germany, Britain, the United States and France, 1780–1914* (Oxford: Blackwell); Simpson, M. (1985), *Thomas Adams and the Modern Planning Movement: Britain, Canada, and the United States, 1900–1940* (London: Mansell); Freestone, R. (ed.) (2000), *Urban Planning in a Changing World: The Twentieth Century Experience* (London: E&FN Spon).

14   Hall, P. (1988), *Cities of Tomorrow: An Intellectual History of Urban Planning and Design in the Twentieth Century* (Oxford: Blackwell); Cherry, G. (1974), *The Evolution of British Town Planning* (London: Leonard Hill).

15   Saunier, P.-Y. (1999), 'Changing the City: Urban International Information and the Lyon Municipality, 1900–1940', *Planning Perspectives* 14: 19–48.

16   Meller, H. (2001), *European Cities 1890–1930s: History, Culture and the Built Environment* (London: Wiley & Sons), 3, 251.

17   See Hein, C. (2014), 'The Exchange of Planning Ideas from Europe to the USA after the Second World War', *Planning Perspectives* 29; Mumford, E. (2000), *The CIAM Discourse on Urbanism, 1928–1960* (Cambridge, MA: MIT Press).

18   Nasr, J. and Volait, M. (eds) (2003), *Urbanism – Imported or Exported? – Native Aspirations and Foreign Plans* (Chichester: John Wiley); Ward, S. V. (2010), 'Transnational Planners in a Postcolonial World', in P. Healey and R. Upton (eds) (2010), *Crossing Borders: International Exchange and Planning* (New York: Routledge), 47–72.

19   Çelik, *Empire, Architecture, and the City*; Lafi, *Municipalités Méditerranéennes*.

20   Kwak, N. H. (2008) 'Selling the City-State: Planning and Housing in Singapore, 1945–1990', in P.-Y. Saunier and S. Ewen (eds), *Another Global City: Historical Explorations into the Transnational Municipal Moment, 1800–2000* (New York: Palgrave), quote at 94.

21 Almandoz, A. (1999), 'Transfer of Urban ideas: The Emergence of Venezuelan Urbanism in the Proposals for 1930s Caracus', *International Planning Studies* 4; 79–94.

22 Griffiths, J. (2009), 'Were There Municipal Networks in the British World *c*.1890–1939?', *The Journal of Imperial and Commonwealth History* 37: 575–97, quote at 581; Griffiths, J. (2008), 'Civic Communication in Britain: A Study of the Municipal Journal *c*.1893–1910', *Journal of Urban History* 34: 775–94.

23 Hietala, M. (1987) *Services and Urbanization at the Turn of the Century: The Diffusion of Innovations* (Helsinki: Societas Historica Finlandiae), 37; Rogers, E. (1983), *Diffusion of Innovations* (New York: Free Press).

24 My own research has been influenced by both authors. See Ewen, S. (2005), 'The Internationalization of Fire Protection: In Pursuit of Municipal Networks in Edwardian Birmingham', *Urban History* 32: 288–307.

25 Rodgers, D. T. (1996), *Atlantic Crossings: Social Politics in a Progressive Age* (New Haven: Harvard University Press), 33–4. Klemek's study of the evolution of an international 'urban renewal order' takes Rodgers's approach as its starting point: *Transatlantic Collapse*, 48. For a recent survey of this literature, see Kwak, N. H. (2008), 'Research in Urban History: Recent Theses on International and Comparative Urban History', *Urban History* 35: 316–25.

26 Rodgers, *Atlantic Crossings*, 132–59; Shaw, A. (1895), *Municipal Government in Great Britain* (London: T. Fisher Unwin); Shaw, A. (1895), *Municipal Government in Continental Europe* (New York: Century).

27 On Harris, see Couperus, S. and Ewen, S. (forthcoming 2015), 'Whose "Urban Internationale"? Intermunicipalism in Europe, *c*.1924–36: The Value of a Decentrist Approach to Transnational Urban History', in Madgin and Kenny (eds), *Comparative and Transnational Approaches to Urban History*.

28 Hietala, *Services and Urbanization*, 361–81.

29 Hietala, *Services and Urbanization*, 394–5.

Suggestions for Further Reading

The following list of suggestions for further reading is indicative of the impressive range and breadth of published research available within the field. It is a selective and subjective choice, but I have tried to give as wide a coverage to the field as possible. The list contains what I consider to be key texts in urban history, as well as recently published texts, in order to provide a more comprehensive overview of the field. Much like the chapters themselves, the reading lists overlap and the reader would benefit from reading across them. The reader should use this list in conjunction with the endnotes to the individual chapters as a starting point for further research.

Chapter 1 The Development of Urban History

The best introductions to the field as a whole remain Dyos, H. J. (ed.) (1968), *The Study of Urban History* (London: Edward Arnold); and Fraser, D. and Sutcliffe, A. S. (eds) (1983), *The Pursuit of Urban History* (London: Edward Arnold). For definitions of key concepts, read Jansen, H. (2001), *The Construction of an Urban Past: Narrative and System in Urban History* (London: Bloomsbury). For a fascinating politicized introduction to US urban history, read

Warner, Jr, S. B. (1972), *The Urban Wilderness: A History of the American City* (New York: Harper & Row). A more general overview of urbanization in America is provided by Brownell, B. A. and Goldfield, D. R. (1990), *Urban America: A History* (Boston: Houghton Mifflin). European urban history is charted in Pinol, J.-L. (ed.) (2003), *Histoire de l'Europe urbaine* (Paris: Seuil), and Clark, P. (2009), *European Cities and Towns, 400–2000* (Oxford: Oxford University Press). The best introduction to Latin American urban history is Almandoz, A. (ed.) (2002), *Planning Latin America's Capital Cities, 1850–1950* (London: Routledge), while Chinese urban history is well served by key historiographical surveys, including Haiyan, L. and Stapleton, K. (2006), 'Chinese Urban History: State of the Field', *China Information* 20: 391–427. There is also a special issue of *Urban History* 38 (2011), guest edited by Toby Lincoln and Liu Haiyan and containing an excellent introductory essay by Jeffrey Wasserstrom. Clark, P. (ed.) (2013), *The Oxford Handbook of Cities in World History* (Oxford: Oxford University Press), contains excellent wide-ranging thematic and geographical essays. There are numerous good recent surveys in the pages of *Urban History* and the *Journal of Urban History*. The annual theses review essay published in *Urban History* since 2008 is a particularly good place to learn about cutting-edge research in an international and comparative context. The reader should also subscribe to H-URBAN for up-to-date electronic discussions of research, and peruse the proceedings of the conferences of the Urban History Group, the Urban History Association, the European Association for Urban History and others, available online, for links to abstracts and other key information.

Chapter 2   Cities, Spaces and Identities

There is a clear overview of the themes and concepts related to the relationship between urban space and social identity, as well as excellent case-study chapters, in Gunn, S. and Morris, R. J. (eds) (2001), *Identities in Space: Contested Terrains in the Western City since 1850* (Aldershot: Ashgate). For a recent global perspective on spatial segregation in cities, see

Nightingale, C. (2012), *Segregation: A Global History of Divided Cities* (Chicago: University of Chicago Press). There is also excellent coverage of urban inequalities in various chapters in Clark, P. (ed.) (2013), *The Oxford Handbook of Cities in World History* (Oxford: Oxford University Press). Freund, B. (2007), *The African City* (Cambridge: Cambridge University Press), contains much of value on issues of inequality in African cities. There are many histories of suburbanization; there is a very good overview of the literature in McManus, R. and Ethington, P. J. (2007), 'Suburbs in Transition: New Approaches to Suburban History', *Urban History* 34: 317–37. For overviews of working-class housing, Daunton, M. J. (ed.) (1990), *Housing the Workers, 1850–1914: A Comparative Perspective* (London: Pinter), provides an international comparative framework. More generally, Rodger, R. (1995), *Housing in Urban Britain 1780–1914* (Cambridge: Cambridge University Press), provides an excellent introduction to the themes, issues and primary sources encountered by historians of housing and urban form. A recent survey of research into the relationship between gender, sexuality and the city is provided by Pluskota, M. (2014), 'Research in Urban History: Recent Ph.D. Theses on Gender and the City, 1550–2000', *Urban History* 41: 537–46. There is also a good overview of the recent historiography on sexuality in American cities by Potter, C. (2014), 'A Queer Public Sphere: Urban History's Sexual Landscape', *Journal of Urban History* 40: 812–22. Some good recent studies of the relationship between race, ethnicity and urban space include Chua, L. (2014), 'The City and the City: Race, Nationalism, and Architecture in Early Twentieth-century Bangkok', *Journal of Urban History* 40: 933–58; and Carnevale, N. C. (2014), 'Italian American and African American Encounters in the City and in the Suburb', *Journal of Urban History* 40: 536–62.

Chapter 3 Governing Cities

There are some excellent overviews on the topics of municipal government and urban governance. Morris, R. J. and Trainor, R. H. (eds) (2000), *Urban Governance: Britain and Beyond since 1750* (Aldershot: Ashgate), includes an excellent introduction by Morris and very good case studies.

Doyle, B. M. (ed.) (2007), *Urban Politics and Space in the Nineteenth and Twentieth Centuries: Regional Perspectives* (Newcastle-upon-Tyne: Cambridge Scholars Press), is more up-to-date. Roth, R. and Beachy, R. (eds) (2007), *Who Ran The Cities? City Elites and Urban Power Structures in Europe and North America, 1750–1940* (Aldershot: Ashgate), has greater international coverage of urban elites. Couperus, S., Smit, C. and Wolffram, D. J. (eds) (2007), *In Control of the City: Local Elites and the Dynamics of Urban Politics, 1800– 1960* (Leuven: Peeters), also provides a broad coverage and includes an important chapter by Simon Gunn, reflecting critically on the concept of urban elites. Municipal workers receive much-needed historiographical attention in Dagenais, M., Maver, I. and Saunier, P.-Y. (eds) (2003), *Municipal Services and Employees in the Modern City: New Historic Approaches* (Aldershot: Ashgate). On the concept and application of civil society, see the essays in Rodger, R. and Colls, R. (eds) (2004), *Cities of Ideas: Civil Society and Urban Governance in Britain 1800–2000* (Aldershot: Ashgate). A good overview of recent doctoral research into urban administrative history is provided by Couperus, S. (2010), 'Research in Urban History: Recent Theses on Nineteenth- and Early Twentieth-century Municipal Administration', *Urban History* 38: 322–32.

Chapter 4   Cities and the Environment

The literature on urban environmental history is fast-growing and increasingly global in its coverage. For excellent recent overviews, see Mosley, S. and Massard-Guilbaud, G. (eds) (2011), *Common Ground: Integrating the Social and Environmental in History* (Newcastle: Cambridge Scholars Publishing), and Massard-Guilbaud, G. and Rodger, R. (eds) (2011), *Environmental and Social Justice in the City: Historical Perspectives* (Cambridge: White Horse Press). There is a very good, and critical, review of recent PhD theses in the field in Frioux, S. (2012), 'At a Green Crossroads: Recent Theses in Urban Environmental History in Europe and North America', *Urban History* 39: 529–39. The literature on urban environmental disasters and reconstruction planning is equally vast, with excellent summaries and case studies available in Vale, L. and Campanella, T. (eds) (2005), *The Resilient City: How Modern Cities Recover from Disaster* (Oxford: Oxford University Press); Bankoff, G., Lübken, U. and Sand, J. (eds) (2012), *Flammable Cities: Urban Conflagration and the Making of the Modern World* (Madison: University of Wisconsin Press); and, most recently, Gotham, K. F. and Greenberg, M. (2014), *Crisis Cities: Disaster and Redevelopment in New York and New Orleans* (New York: Oxford University Press). Page, M. (2010), *The City's End: Two Centuries of Fantasies, Fears, and Premonitions of New York's Destruction* (New Haven: Yale University Press), is a hugely entertaining cultural history of urban destruction by environmental catastrophe, alien invasion and giant apes.

Chapter 5   Urban Culture and Modernity

The most well-known study of urban modernity is Harvey, D. (2005), *Paris, Capital of Modernity* (London: Routledge). There is a very good overview of the key theorists and texts in Gunn, S. (2006), *History and Cultural Theory* (Harlow: Pearson). Gunn has also co-edited, with Alastair Owens, a special issue of *Cultural Geographies* 13 (2006) on 'Nature, Technology and the Modern City' with engaging essays by Matthew Gandy, Chris Otter, Leif Jerram and others. There are excellent studies of modernity in Indian cities, including Chopra, P. (2011), *A Joint Enterprise: Indian Elites and the Making of British Bombay* (Minneapolis: University of Minnesota Press), and Chattopadhyay, S. (2005), *Representing Calcutta: Modernity, Nationalism and the Colonial Uncanny* (London: Routledge). Esherick, J. W. (ed.) (2000), *Remaking the Chinese City: Modernity and National Identity, 1900–1950* (Honolulu: University of Hawai'i Press), contains excellent chapters on Chinese urban modernity, notably by Madeleine Yue Dong, Ruth Rogaski and Kristin Stapleton. Hanes, J. E. (2002), *The City as Subject: Seki Hajime and the Reinvention of Modern Osaka* (Berkeley: University of California Press), examines the relationship between a single urban elite and urban modernity. Jerram, L. (2011), *Streetlife: The Untold History of Europe's Twentieth Century* (Oxford: Oxford University Press), examines the everyday histories of

European city-dwellers during a tumultuous century of economic and political change, while Gandy, M. (2014), *The Fabric of Space: Water, Modernity, and the Urban Imagination* (Cambridge, MA: MIT Press), examines the relationship between nature, modernity and the city through a global lens.

Chapter 6   Transnational Urban History

The best introduction to transnational history is Sauier, P.-Y. (2013), *Transnational History* (New York: Palgrave). Saunier has also edited, along with Akira Iriye (2009), *The Palgrave Dictionary of Transnational History* (New York: Palgrave), with many relevant entries on urban history topics. Rodgers, D. T. (1996), *Atlantic Crossings: Social Politics in a Progressive Age* (New Haven: Harvard University Press), should be read alongside Klemek, C. (2011), *The Transatlantic Collapse of Urban Renewal: Postwar Urbanism from New York to Berlin* (Chicago: University of Chicago Press), for a long-term insight into transatlantic planning exchanges. There are some interesting recent articles on the international and transnational dimensions of post-war urban renewal, including those in the special issue of *Planning Perspectives* 29, edited by Carola Hein, on 'The Exchange of Planning Ideas from Europe to the USA after the Second World War'; and a special forum of the *Journal of Urban History* 40, coordinated by Alexander von Hoffman, on 'Urban Renewal'. Madgin, R. and Kenny, N. (eds) (2015), *Comparative and Transnational Approaches to Urban History: Cities beyond Borders* (Aldershot: Ashgate), contains cutting-edge research on various aspects of transnational urban history, with a wider geographic and temporal coverage. There are also many relevant chapters, and an excellent introduction, in Saunier, P.-Y. and Ewen, S. (eds) (2008), *Another Global City: Historical Explorations into the Transnational Municipal Moment, 1850–2000* (New York: Palgrave). Kwak, N. H. (2008), 'Research in Urban History: Recent Theses on International and Comparative Urban History', *Urban History* 35: 316–25, provides an excellent overview of recent PhD completions in the field, some of which have since gone on to be published as monographs.

Index

activism, 17–18, 28, 32, 53–4,
    105–6
acts of God, 89
    see also disasters
Africa
    housing standards in Angola
        and the Congo, 47
    residential segregation by
        ethnicity, 49–50
    shortage of toilets, 52
    South Africa, rise of urban
        history, 28
    transience in Zambia's
        Copperbelt, 45
    urban history, 30
    urbanization, 4
Ahnlund, Nils, 16
AIDS crisis, 103
Almandoz, Arturo, 96, 122–3
ambulances, 83
ancient city, 8, 15, 107–8
Annales School and urban
        history, 2, 11
anthropocene, 77
anthropology, 1
    and transnational
        history, 114–15

and urban history, 29, 34,
    63
antiquarianism, 12
anti-urbanism, 14, 38–9
Appadurai, Arjun, 114
archaeology and urban
        history, 2, 77
architects, 18, 28, 74, 96, 97,
        104, 107
architecture, 18–19, 31, 43,
        95, 99–100, 107–8
    and urban history, 26–7, 32,
        100
    styles of urban
        architecture, 26, 71–2,
        95–6, 103–5
art and urban history, 2, 24
arts and humanities, 2, 10–11,
        14–15, 24–5, 32
Asia
    threat of fire, 89
    urbanization, 4
    see also China; India;
        Middle East; Ottoman
        Empire
associations, *see* voluntary
        associations

Australia
  gay suburban
    communities, 44
  municipal officials, 123
  suburban ideal, 39
automobile, 18, 37–8, 97,
    100–1, 103–4, 121

Bairoch, Paul, 7
Bankoff, Greg, 89–90
banlieues, 40
bars, 102–3
Bateman, John Frederic la
    Trobe (Manchester), 82
baths, 112, 127
Baudelaire, Charles, 94, 109
Bayly, Christopher, 118
beaches, 111
Beaux-Arts, 96
Beck, Ulrich, 114
Beckert, Sven, 118
Benjamin, Walter, 14, 94, 109
Berman, Marshall, 94
bidonvilles, 46
Blatchford, Robert, 14
Bloomingdale's (New
    York), 101
Blumenfeld, Hans, 104
Blumin, Stuart, 26
boards of trade, 65
Boyar, Ebru, 66
Boyle Heights (Los
    Angeles), 104
brass bands, 65
Braudel, Fernand, 11
Brazil
  FIFA World Cup host
    (2014), 76
  slum districts, 47
  urban protests, 75–6
  women in *favelas*, 53–4
breweries, 88
bridges, 63, 68, 98, 108
Briggs, Asa, 25
Britain

Association of Municipal
    Corporations (UK), 57
  garden cities, 13
  gender and provincial
    culture, 41–2
  imperial connections, 39,
    123
  liberal governmentality, 71–2
  middle-class culture, 95–6
  municipal
    government, 57–62, 64,
    68–9, 125–7
  new towns, 122
  post-war planning, 105–6
  residential segregation, 36–7,
    38, 39–40
  rise of industrial
    cities, 13–14
  shopkeepers, 60
  urban history, 10–11, 20–2,
    27, 57
  voluntary associations,
    65–7
  waterworks, 127
British Committee for the
    Study of Foreign
    Innovations, 127
Brodrick, Cuthbert, 96
  see also Leeds Town Hall
bubonic plague, 50
  see also disease; public
    health
builders, 21, 35–41, 42–3,
    47–52
  see also property developers
building controls, 51–2
Burgess, Ernest W., 16
Burgess model, 37–8
Burgh Police (Scotland) Act
    (1833), 58
  see also municipal
    government;
    municipalization
Burke, Peter, 37
Butes (Cardiff), 38

Calthorpes (Birmingham), 38
Cannadine, David, 36, 38
capital cities, 8, 23, 40, 94–5,
　113
　see also individual capital
　cities; typologies of cities
cartography, 71, 93
casinos, 103
casual labour, 45, 51
　see also urban poor
Çelik, Zeynep, 122
census, 40, 58
Central Park (New York), 112
Centre for Urban History,
　University of Leicester, 21
Certeau, Michel de, 93
Chamberlain, Joseph
　(Birmingham), 59, 74
Chandler, Tertius, 5
charity, *see* philanthropy
Checkland, Sydney, 22–3
chemical works, 88
cheongzhongcun ('villages-in-
　the-city') (China), 48
Cherry, Gordon, 119
Chesbrough, Ellis
　(Chicago), 82
Chicago School, 16–17
child labour, 45
China
　capital city, 108
　Civil War (1946–9), 47,
　　108
　disasters, 89
　megacities, 3
　municipal government in
　　Republican China,
　　62–3
　Sino–Japanese War
　　(1937–45), 47
　urban history, 6, 30–1
Chopra, Preeti, 107
churches, 45, 65, 96
Churchill, David, 112–13
cinemas, 38, 99, 102

cities and towns, as objects for
　study, 11–12, 16–17
Abu Dhabi, 97, 99
Accra, 6
Adelaide, 39
Algiers, 97, 107
Amsterdam, 62
Atlanta, 106
Atlantic City, 102–3
Baghdad, 83–4
Balıkesir (Turkey), 66
Bangalore, 6
Bangkok, 103
Barcelona, 106
Beijing/Beiping, 5, 48, 107–8
Beirut, 97
Berlin, 5, 15, 40, 93, 94, 99,
　109–10, 121
Bhopal, 52
Birmingham, 36, 38, 46,
　57–60, 61, 95, 120, 125–6
Bloomington, Indiana, 25
Bolton, 60
Bombay/Mumbai, 5, 6,
　29–30, 45, 50, 106–7
Boston, Massachusetts, 26,
　35–6, 68, 84–5
Bradford, 103
Brazzaville, 47
Bristol, 68–9
Budapest, 94, 99, 108,
　120
Buenos Aires, 5, 40, 96
Cairo, 6, 96–7, 102, 107
Calcutta/Kolkata, 5, 50,
　106
Cape Town, 50, 106
Caracas, 122–3
Cardiff, 38
Chicago, 5, 16–17, 26, 40,
　49, 79–81, 82–5, 94, 116
Chorley, Lancashire, 36
Cologne, 106
Columbus, Ohio, 17
Constantinople, 5

Coventry, 40
Damascus, 97
Delhi, 6, 52
Detroit, 41, 49
Doha, 97
Dubai, 97, 99
Düsseldorf, 15
Edinburgh, 33, 38, 66–7, 90
Exeter, 36
Fez, 107
Frankfurt, 64
Freetown, 50
Ghent, 16
Glasgow, 38, 125
Hamburg, 120
Hobart, 39
Holmfirth, West
   Yorkshire, 83, 90
Ibadan, 6
Istanbul, 62, 96–7
Kanpur, 51
Kiev, 106
Kuala Lumpur, 103
Lagos, 6
Leeds, 38, 57–60, 65, 95,
   99
Leicester, 73
Lincoln, 36
Liverpool, 40
London, 5, 6, 33, 35–6, 45,
   94, 101, 112–13
Los Angeles, 40, 90, 103–4,
   116
Lourenço Marques/
   Maputo, 50
Luanda, 47
Lusaka, 45
Lyons, 55, 120
Manchester, 36, 82, 83, 94,
   95, 105, 125–5
Manila, 48, 89–90
Marseilles, 120
Melbourne, 39, 101–2
Memphis, 106
Merthyr Tydfil, 72

Mexico City, 5, 6, 33, 48,
   96, 103
Milan, 40, 103
Montevideo, 96
Montreal, 40
Moscow, 110
Nairobi, 52
Nanjing, 108
Nashville, 106
Newburyport,
   Massachusetts, 20
New Orleans, 83
New York City, 5, 26, 33,
   43–4, 46, 56, 86–8, 99,
   100, 101, 106, 112, 116
Norwich, 60, 62
Nottingham, 61–2
Odessa, 110–11
Oldham, Lancashire, 60
Osaka, 62
Paris, 5, 14, 40, 45, 48–9,
   94–5, 96, 101, 109, 122
Perth, Western Australia, 39
Philadelphia, 40, 84–5, 106
Prague, 120
Rabat (106)
Rio de Janeiro, 5, 6, 47, 52,
   53–4, 75–6, 106
Rochdale, Lancashire, 60
Rome, 122
St Petersburg, 97–8, 109–10
San Francisco, 44, 90
San José do Costa Rica, 40
São Paulo, 5, 6, 47
Seoul-Injon, 48
Shanghai, 5, 30–1, 47, 63,
   106
Sheffield, 83, 90, 105
Singapore, 122
Stockholm, 40
Swansea, 61
Sydney, 39, 44, 46
Tehran, 90, 96
Tianjin, 31
Tokyo, 5, 93

cities and towns, as objects for
    study (cont.)
  Toronto, 40, 112–13
  Tripoli, 62
  Tunis, 62
  Vienna, 33, 48, 94–5, 99,
    101, 120
  Washington, DC, 122
city beautiful movement, 40, 42
city biography, 12, 22–3
city centres, 95–6, 98–9,
    100–1, 108, 111
  see also downtown
city rankings, 5, 15
civic identity, 15, 18, 59, 65–6,
    87, 95–9, 113
civil society, 63–7, 73–4
Clark, Peter, 1, 6
class approaches to urban
    history, 8, 13–14, 20,
    24–6, 33–54, 64–5,
    89–90, 94–6, 101–2,
    104–6, 109–10, 111
climate change, 75
clock towers, 45, 96–7
Closed Circuit Television
    (CCTV), 73
clubs and societies, 58, 65
  see also voluntary
    associations; and
    individual clubs
coffee shops, 31
Cohen, William, 55
Cold War, 99–100, 121
colonial cities and
    societies, 28–30, 35, 39,
    49–53, 89–90, 96–7,
    106–7, 121–3
comparative approaches to the
    city, 1–6, 20–4, 35–41,
    46–51, 57–64, 68–9, 73–4,
    81–6, 115–16, 120–1
Congrès Internationaux
    d'architecture moderne
    (CIAM), 121

Conzen, Kathleen, 20
Corfield, Penelope, 3, 61
council housing estates, 40
  Hulme Crescents,
    Manchester, 105
  Kingstanding,
    Birmingham, 120–1
  Park Hill, Sheffield, 105
  Villeurbanne, Lyons, 120–1
countryside and the city, 8,
    10–11, 79
courts, 15, 53
Croll, Andy, 72
Cronon, William, 78, 79–80
Crossick, Geoffrey, 60
Croton Aqueduct (New
    York), 87
cultural attitudes towards
    cities, 13–14, 24–8,
    30–1, 46–7, 53, 85–8,
    92–113
cultural history, 12, 34
  and urban history, 7, 24–8,
    46–7, 93–4
cultural studies, 2, 28–9

dancing halls, 31, 112
dangers of urban life, 42,
    52–3, 98–100, 102–3,
    110–13
Darwin, Charles, 15
Davidoff, Leonore, 41–2
Davis, Mike, 48
Davison, Graeme, 39
degeneration, 13–14, 51
de-industrialization, 7, 102–3,
    106
Dennis, Richard, 40
department stores, 95, 96–8,
    99, 100–2, 111
destruction of cities, 18,
    79–80, 83–4, 90, 94–5,
    97–8, 100, 121, 133
  see also reconstruction of
    cities

Dickens, Charles, 109
DiGaetano, Alan, 68, 74
disasters, 83–4, 89–90, 100
  see also earthquakes; fires;
    floods; natural disasters
disease, including fear
  of, 29–30, 49–53, 87
domestic space, 41–4, 103
domestic workers, 45
Domosh, Mona, 27
Dong, Madeleine Yue, 107–8
Dostoevsky, Fedor, 109
downtown, 18–19, 100–1,
  104
  see also city centres
Doyle, Barry, 60, 61–2
Dyos, H. J., 10, 20–2, 24–5,
  35–6, 46

early modern city, 8, 68, 73,
  84
earthquakes, 89, 90
ecology, 75, 77, 89–91
economic and social history, 2,
  7
  and urban history, 11–12,
    12–20, 25
economics, 14–15, 88
  and transnational
    history, 115, 118
ecosystems, 78
Edinburgh Society for the
  Suppression of
  Begging, 66
Edwards, Samuel
  (Birmingham), 59
electricity, 46, 53, 59,
  127
elite(s), 26–7
  and their relationship with
    the urban poor, 29–31,
    45–6
  and space, 95–8
  and urban governance,
    68–70, 73–4

and urban
  government, 55–65
  as technocrats, 103–4,
    122–3
  as transnational
    reformers, 123–8
emotions, history of the, 74
engineering, 76, 83, 84–6,
  107, 126–7
engineers, 71, 74, 82, 87–8,
  96, 107, 115
  see also individual engineers
environmental footprint of
  cities, 3–5, 75–6, 78–81,
  82–5, 87–91
environmental history, 6, 32,
  72, 77–81
environmental justice, 4, 6,
  11–12, 15
ethnicity, 4, 20, 24–6, 33–41,
  44–54, 90, 98, 104–5,
  107
  see also race; racism
Europe
  critics of post-war
    architecture, 19
  planned suburbanization, 40
  urban history in Eastern
    Europe, 30
  urban history in Western
    Europe, 6, 13
  urbanization, 12
European Association for
  Urban History
  (EAUH), 27–8, 115
  see also scholarly networks
exhibitions, 15–16, 26
expertise, 17–18, 55–8, 61–2,
  71–2, 103–4, 123–8

factories, 36, 40–1, 45, 96,
  106, 111
factory workers, 40–1, 44–5,
  see also urban poor
Falck, Zachary, 86

Falkus, Malcolm, 73
favelas, 46–7, 53, 106
Ferguson, James, 45
Fernsehturm (Berlin TV
    Tower), 99–100
feuilletonist, 109–10
film-making, 31, 81, 110–11
film studies, 2
financiers, 21, 33–4
Finland
    local government, 126–6
    urban history, 16
fire-fighting services, 55, 56,
    59, 68, 69, 73, 83, 87, 88,
    90, 108, 110, 127
fires, 80–1, 88–90, 98, 110
Fischer, Brodwyn, 35, 50–4
flâneur, 98, 108–13
floods, 83–4, 90
Ford, President Gerald
    (USA), 48
fossil fuels, 77
Foucault, Michel, 70
fountains, 66, 87
Fox, Gerald, 5
France
    industrial cities, 13–14
    private property, 49
    provincial municipal
        government, 55–6
    urban history, 13, 27
Fraser, Derek, 22
freeways, 19, 97, 103
friendly societies, 65
Frioux, Stéphane, 88
Frost, Lionel, 89
Furnée, Jan Hein, 67

gambling, 103
Gandy, Matthew, 29–30, 86–8
garden cities, 13, 40, 42, 123
gardening clubs, 65
Garrard, John, 60
gas, gas stations, 38, 59, 61,
    69, 125, 127

gay clubs, 102–3
Geddes, Patrick, 42
Geertz, Clifford, 63
gender, 8, 24–6, 34, 41–4,
    52–3, 101–2, 108–13,
    121
    see also history of
        masculinity
gentrification, 106
geography, 1, 16–17, 19, 34,
    76, 115
geology, 77
Germany
    burgher (middle)
        classes, 64–5
    burgomaster, 56
    example of municipal
        government, 126–7
    industrial cities, 13–14
    urban history, 10, 13, 27
Ghent Exposition Universelle
    (1913), 16
Gieryn, Thomas, 17
Gilfoyle, Timothy, 26
Glaeser, Edwin, 88
global history, 116–17
    see also international history;
        transnational history;
        world history
globalization, 7, 29, 75–6, 77,
    99–100
    and transnational
        history, 114–18
    and urban environmental
        history, 89–91
    and urban history, 2–3,
        23–4
Goffman, Jean, 18
Goldberger, Paul, 100
Gooptu, Nandini, 45, 52
governance, 4, 55–7, 64–70,
    80–1
government, *see* municipal
    government
governmentality, 57, 70–4

grain stores, 79–80
Griffiths, John, 123
Gropius, Walter, 104
guidebooks, 108, 109
guilds, 65, 66
Gunn, Simon, 34, 95–6

Hajime, Seiki (Osaka), 62–3
Hall, Catherine, 41–2
Hall, Sir Peter, 88, 119
Handlin, Oscar, 19
Hansen, Georg, 14
harbours, 63
Harris, George Montagu, 126
Harris, Richard, 40–1
Haupt, Heinz-Gerhard, 60
Haussmann, Georges-
    Eugène, 40, 49, 95, 109
Haussmannization, 96–7,
    107–8
hawkers, 45, 102
    see also urban poor
Hayden, Dolores, 11
Hayes, Nick, 61–2
Hein, Carola, 24
Hennock, E. P., 57–60, 63, 65,
    74
Henriot, Christian, 63
Heriot, George, 67
heritage, 107–8
Herlitz, Nils, 16
Herriot, Edouard, 55, 74
Hietala, Marjatta, 123–4,
    126–8
historical sociology, 2
history of masculinity, 41
history of technology, 72,
    81–2, 84–6
Hobsbawm, Eric, 11
Hodge, Stephen, 44
Hollow, Matthew, 105
homosexuality, 44, 102–3,
    111–13
    see also sexuality
Hong, Ho–Fung 7

horses, 37, 38, 82–3, 96, 110
hospitals, 56, 64, 127
    see also ambulances; public
    health
Hotel Stadt Berlin, 100
hotels, 50, 99, 100, 102
Houlbrook, Matt, 112–13
housing, 33–4, 35–9, 40–1,
    42–3, 45–52, 56, 75,
    89–90, 105–6, 120–2
    council housing, 40, 61–2,
    105, 120–1
    high-rise, 18, 33, 40, 97, 99,
    105–6
    and slum clearance, 48–52
    see also council housing
    estates; suburbia; suburbs;
    slums
H-Urban, 32
Hüsseyin, Elhaç, 66

identity, *see* class; ethnicity;
    gender; nationalism;
    religion; sexuality
immigration, 12, 34–5, 38–41,
    50
    see also migration to cities
India
    engineering and
    planning, 107
    improvement trusts, 50–2
    megacities, 3
    public architecture, 107
    residential segregation and
    housing reform, 50–2
    shortage of toilets, 52–3
    urban history, 6, 28–30
    urbanization, 28
Indian Ocean tsunami
    (2004), 83
industrial cities, 12–14, 16–17,
    19–23, 26–7, 35–41, 45,
    56–63, 65–6, 68–74,
    79–88, 94–6, 126–7
    see also typologies of cities

industrialization, 12–13, 16,
    21, 38, 50, 75–8
industrial
    suburbanization, 40–1
    see also suburbanization
inequality in cities, 4–5,
    18–19, 29, 34–5, 44–54,
    75–6
    see also environmental
    justice; segregation; social
    justice
Institute of Civil Engineers
    (UK), 107
Institute of Urban History
    (Sweden), 16
insurance companies, insurance
    industry, 27, 88
interdisciplinarity and urban
    history, 1–8, 10–12,
    16–27, 28–30
    and environmental
    history, 76–7
    and planning history, 119
    and transnational
    history, 114–16
International Federation of
    Housing and Town
    Planning (IFHTP), 121
international history, 117–18
    see also global history;
    transnational history;
    world history
International Labour
    Organisation, 122
International Planning History
    Society (IPHS), 115
    see also planning history;
    scholarly networks
Isenberg, Alison, 100
Islamic city, 66, 122
Italy
    urban history, 27

Jackson, Kenneth, 37–8, 43
Jacobs, Jacobs, 18, 79, 104

James, Henry, 109
Japan
    Meiji municipal
    government, 62–3
    urbanization, 12
jazz clubs, 31
journalists, 28, 32, 45, 46,
    109–10
journals and periodicals:
    *American Historical
    Review*, 117–18
    Architectural Review, 19
    Bauwelt, 19
    *Journal of Urban
    History*, 20, 24, 30, 79
    Municipal Journal, 123
    Review of Reviews, 125
    Urban History, 20, 24,
    27–8, 30, 32
    *Urban History
    Newsletter*, 20
    *Urban History Review /
    Revue d'histoire
    urbaine*, 24
    *Urban History
    Yearbook*, 20, 27
Joyce, Patrick, 71–2, 147 fn.
    31

Kaika, Maria, 86
Kelly, Barbara, 43
Kidambi, Prashant, 29
Klemek, Christopher, 18, 104
Koch, Ed (New York), 56, 74
Kōjirō, Hirade, 109
Kwak, Nancy, 122

labourers, labouring
    classes, 44–5, 51–2, 53
    see also class; urban poor
Lafi, Nora, 122
Lampard, Eric, 17
landlords, 33–4, 46, 49, 128
landowners, 21, 38
landownership, 36

Latin America
  megacities, 3
  urban history, 6, 30
  urban planning, 40, 96
Lawton, Richard, 39
Le Bon Marché (Paris), 96,
  101
Le Corbusier, 103, 105, 121
  see also architects;
    modernism; planners
Leeds Improvement Act
  (1842), 59
Leeds Town Hall, 96
Lees, Andrew, 13–14
leisure, 26, 45, 96–9, 101–2,
  108–13
Levasseur, Emile, 14
Lewis, Robert, 40
libraries, 65
linguistic turn, 25–7, 46–7, 70
  see also cultural history
literary and philosophical
  societies, 65
local history, 12, 78
locksmiths, 66
Low Countries
  municipal government in
    Amsterdam, 62
  urban history, 10, 13, 27
  voluntarism, 67
Lu, Hanchao, 47
lumber, lumber yards, 79, 80,
  81

McFarland, J. Horace, 42
McKelvey, Blake, 17
mahalles, 66
  see also neighbourhoods
Man With A Movie Camera
  (1929), 110–11
mapping, maps, 24, 71,
  109–10
markets, 15, 66
market sellers, 45
market towns, 30

Marx, Karl, 94
Marxist tradition of
  history, 25
materiality of cities, 2, 6,
  26–7, 31, 56–7, 70–2,
  76, 84–8, 100–4,
  109–10
  see also governmentality
Mauch, Christof, 89
May, Andrew, 101–2
Mayne, Alan, 46, 53
mayors, 48, 55–6, 62, 63, 69,
  127
  see also individual mayors
meat-packing industry
  (Chicago), 79, 81
mechanics institutes, 65
medieval city, 8, 13, 40, 66,
  83–4
Mediterranean cities, 11, 23
mega-cities, 3, 5, 8, 23, 31
megalopolis, 18, 29
mega-regions, 3, 6, 18, 45
Meller, Helen 120
Melosi, Martin, 76, 78
memorials, 97, 100
merchants, merchant
  elites, 59–60, 63, 67,
  68–9, 99, 108
Mesopotamia, 84
metropolis, 5, 56, 88, 92–5,
  106–10
Meuriot, Paul, 14
Mexico, urban disasters, 89
middle-class flight, 102
Middle East
  city skylines, 97
  comparison with Western
    City, 15
  megacities, 3
  modernization, 96–7
  urban history, 30
migration to cities, 5, 8, 14,
  48–9, 53, 61
Ming dynasty (China), 30

Ministry of Housing and Local Government (UK), 57
Miskell, Louise, 61
Miss Universe (1974), 48
Mitter, Rana, 30
modernism, 103–5, 120
modernity, 7, 13–15, 30–1, 87, 92–113, 122
modernization, 10–11, 31, 62–3, 94–7
Monkkonen, Eric, 20
Moore, James, 61
Morris, R. J., 64–5, 66–7
multimedia, 32
multi-storey car parks, 103
Mumbai Studies Group, 28
Mumford, Lewis, 18–19
Municipal Corporations Act (1835) (UK), 58, 61, 68
municipal government, 55–64, 67–70, 71–4, 122–3, 125–8
  see also municipalization; public services
municipalization, 13, 21, 31, 59, 67, 124–7
municipal officials, 31, 46, 56–7, 61–3, 71–2, 85–6, 106, 123–6
Murzban, Khan Bahadur Muncherji Cowasji (Bombay), 107
museums, 81, 149 fn. 18
music hall, 111

National Housing Act (1934) (USA), 37
nationalism, nationalist, 26, 29, 108, 115
nation-states, 14, 75–6, 114–18, 123–5
natural disasters, 89–90
nature, in cities, 3, 13, 77–81, 83–8
Nead, Lynda, 101

necropolis, 18
neighbourhoods, 18, 62, 66, 104–6
Nettlefold, John (Birmingham), 59
Nevskii Prospect (St Petersburg), 97–8
'New Brutalism', 105
newspapers, newspaper industry, 27, 46, 53, 58, 67, 71, 109–10, 112–13
New Zealand
  municipal officials, 123
North America
  American Social Science Research Council, 19
  city boosterism, 81, 104–5
  civic pride, 87
  critics of post-war planning, 18–19
  downtown, 100–1
  forest fires, 81
  gender and social morphology, 43
  hinterlands, 79–80
  industrial cities, 13–14, 79–81
  municipal government, 68–9, 126
  neighbourhood preservation, 106
  progressive reformers, 124–6
  residential segregation, 37–9, 40–1
  segregation by ethnicity, 33, 34, 40–1, 49
  skyscrapers, 26–7
  urban history, 6, 10, 16–20, 28
  urbanization, 12
  urban renewal, 122
  urban technical infrastructures, 84–8
  US exceptionalism, 125

Norway
  urban history, 16
novelists, 29, 109–10
nuisances, 61, 71

old people's homes, 127
Olsen, Donald, 95
Olympic Games (1988,
  2008), 48, (2016), 76
opera, opera houses, 31, 95,
  96
Otter, Chris, 72, 147 fn. 31
Ottoman Empire, cities of
  the, 62, 96–7, 122
overcrowding, 13, 26, 45–6,
  48–9, 50–1

Park, Robert, 16
Parker, George, 125
parks, 56, 61, 96, 111–12
pedestrians, 93, 104
pedlars, 45
philanthropy, 13, 64–5, 67,
  81, 84, 107, 111
Philippines
  disasters, 89–90
Philo, Chris, 86
photographs, photography, 2,
  24
Pirenne, Henri, 13, 16
planners, 18–19, 42, 93,
  103–4, 119, 121–3
planning history, 32, 119–28
Platt, Harold, 49, 82
playgrounds, 56
police, 31, 53, 55, 56, 59, 61,
  63, 68, 72, 98, 102
policymaking, influence of
  urban historians, 3–5,
  17–19, 32, 35–6, 79,
  91
political science and urban
  history, 19, 57, 115,
  126
Pollard, Sidney, 11

pollution, pollution
  abatement, 38, 71, 75,
  82–3, 88
Pooley, Colin, 40
poor relief, 63, 66, 68, 127
population increase, 3–5, 77,
  85, 87, 97–8, 99
  see also urbanization
port cities, 23–4, 120
post-colonial cities, 28–9,
  120–3
  see also colonial cities and
  societies
post-modern culture, 25, 70,
  72
poverty, *see* urban poor
Power, Nellie (London), 111
prairie cities, 23
Prakash, Gyan, 28
pre-industrial city; *see* ancient
  city; medieval city; Sjoberg
  model
Pre-Modern Towns Group
  (UK), 27
primary sources (types), 46,
  58, 77, 99, 122, 123
property developers and
  owners, 15, 21–2, 25,
  33–4, 48–54, 67, 89–90,
  99
prostitutes, 98, 102
protest, 75–6, 100–1, 106
publicans, 60
public health, 55–6, 59–60,
  68–9, 71–2, 84–8, 122–3
  and urban history, 82–3,
  88
public services, 46, 53, 55–6,
  57–8, 59, 63, 66, 67–8,
  119–20, 124–7
public squares
  Alexanderplatz, 100
  Al-Marjeh, 97
  Place d'Armes, 97
  Place Hamidiyyeh, 97

public toilets, 31, 51, 101–2

Qing dynasty (China), 30

race, 13, 25, 26, 34, 40–1, 100
racism, 49–50
railroads, *see* trams
railway companies, 108
railway stations, 95
railways, 36, 37, 71
rape, 52
Rappaport, Erika, 101
ratepayers, 15, 59–60, 64–5, 69, 85
reconstruction of cities, 17–18, 42, 80, 94–5, 98, 132–3
  see also destruction of cities
Reeder, David, 7, 23, 46
regeneration, 99
religion, 8, 42, 56, 59, 64, 66
rental market, 33–4, 36, 45–6, 48–9, 51, 66
resilience, 83–4
restaurants, 50, 102
Ringstrasse (Vienna), 95
riots, 106
rivers, 84–5
  Schuylkill, 85
  Tigris, 83
roads, 63, 68, 95, 103–4
Robson, William A., 19
Roche, Daniel, 13
Rodger, Richard, 7, 8, 23, 27, 46, 61
Rodgers, Daniel, 123–6, 128
Rogaski, Ruth, 31
Rogers, Everett, 124
roller-skating, 50
Rosen, Christine Meisner, 79–81
Roth, Ralf, 64–5
Royal Institute of British Architects (RIBA), 107
rural life, 11, 13

Russia
  modernization, 97–8
  Russian National Library (St. Petersburg), 98
  Soviet everyday life, 110–11
  Soviet film, 110–11
  urbanization, 12

sanitation, 13, 29–30, 46, 49, 50–3, 56, 71, 122, 126
  see also public health
Saunier, Pierre-Yves, 116–17
Sawislak, Karen, 80
Schlesinger, Sr, Arthur, 17
schools, 45, 56, 67, 68
scholarly networks, 12, 19–20, 21–2, 24–5, 27–9, 32, 116, 118–19
second cities, 23
Seed, Patricia, 118
segregation, 4, 6, 18–19, 21–2, 29–31, 33–54, 92–3, 98–9
Sellers, Jeffry, 115, 116
Senckenberg, Johann, 64
Sert, José Luís, 121
sexuality, 4, 8, 24, 25, 34, 41–4, 110–13
shanty towns, 47, 49, 51
  Fangualong (Shanghai), 47
  Kibera (Nairobi), 52
  Mathee A4 (Nairobi), 52
  Yaoshuilong (Shanghai), 47, 106
  Zhaojiabang (Shanghai), 47
  see also slums
Sharp, Evelyn (UK), 57, 61, 63
Shaw, Albert, 125–6
shopgirls, 101
shopkeepers, 'shopocracy', 60, 67
shoppers, shopping, 19, 38, 101–3, 111
Shoshkes, Ellen, 104
Simmel, Georg, 14, 94, 109

Simms, G. R., 109
Simon, Bryant, 102–3
Singapore Housing and
    Development Board,
    122
Sjoberg, Gideon, 19
Sjoberg model, 37
Skinner, G. William, 30
skyscrapers, 26–7, 97, 99
Sky Tower (Dubai), 99
slaughterhouses, 127
slum clearance, 48–52
slums, 21, 29, 34, 36, 44–54,
    75, 106, 108
slum tourism, 53
Smith, Carl, 80, 84–5
Smith, Michael Peter, 114
Smithson, Alison and
    Peter, 105
social justice, 4, 75–6, 88
    see also environmental
    justice; inequality in
    cities
social media, 32, 81
social mobility, 20, 34, 47
social reformers, 45, 51,
    124–6
social sciences, 2, 10, 14–17,
    24–5, 32, 109–10
Society for American City and
    Regional Planning History
    (SACRPH),
    116
    see also scholarly networks
sociology, 1
    and transnational
    history, 114–15,
    124–5
    and urban history, 2–3,
    16–19, 37, 44, 57, 92–3,
    109
'socionature', 86–7
space and cities, 6, 18, 21,
    29–30, 33–54, 94–102,
    108–13

statistical approaches to urban
    history, 14, 15, 19–20,
    25, 71
Stave, Bruce, 10, 20
Stead, W. T., 109
steam engines, 85
Steffl, 96, 101
Steinberg, Mark, 98
Still, Bayrd, 17
street begging, 66, 102
street cleaning, 55, 63
street fire hydrants, 73
street lighting, 55, 63, 68, 73,
    96
'streets in the sky', 105–6
    see also council housing
    estates; modernism; 'New
    Brutalism'
street, the, 18, 93, 95–8,
    100–1, 102–6, 109–11
street vendors, 45
Strong-Boag, Veronica, 44
sub-letting, 36
suburban sprawl, 18
suburban studies, 35
suburbanization, 21–2, 35–41,
    82–3, 100–1, 131
suburbia, 18–19, 21–2, 34,
    35–44, 46, 48–9, 54,
    90
suburbs:
    Blythswood (Glasgow), 38
    Camberwell (South
    London), 35–6
    Castro (San Francisco), 44
    Chapeltown (Leeds), 38
    Chestnut Hill
    (Philadelphia), 40
    Darlinghurst (Sydney), 44
    Edbgaston (Birmingham), 38
    Greenwich Village (New
    York), 44
    Headingley (Leeds), 38
    Hill Station
    (Freetown), 49–50

suburbs (cont.)
  Levittown (New York
    State), 43
  Near North (Chicago), 40
  New Town (Edinburgh), 38
  New Town (Montreal), 40
suicide, 108
sustainable development, 75,
  79
Sutcliffe, Anthony, 22
Sweden
  Confederation of Swedish
    Towns, 16
  local government, 126–7
  urban history, 16
Sweet, Rosemary, 8, 61
Swyngedouw, Erik, 86

tanneries, 88
Tanzimat, 96–7
  see also Ottoman Empire
Tarr, Joel A., 76, 79–81, 84
temperance societies, 65
tenants, 96
terrorism, 99–100
The Landmark (Dubai), 99
Thernstrom, Stephan, 20
Tilly, Charles, 2
time, 14, 45, 94, 97
time discipline, 96
toilets, 49, 52–3
tourism, 102–3, 108
town halls, 45, 71, 95–6
trade directories, 58, 71
trade unions, 56, 65
traffic architecture, 103–4
traffic signals, 73, 103
Trainor, Richaard, 60
trams (railroads), 37, 59,
  125
translocal, 114
transnational history, 7,
  114–28
transnationalism, 114–19
typologies of cities, 3, 23–4

typologies of suburbs, 39–41
Tyrwhitt, Jaqueline, 104, 121

UN-HABITAT, 3–5, 7, 18
Union Internationale des Villes
  (UIV), 121
United Nations, 121, 122
United Nations Earth Summit
  (1992, 2012), 75
University of Chicago, 16, 19
University of Leicester, 20–1
Unwin, Raymond, 42
urban agglomerations, 5, 14
urban conservation, 17
urban corridors, 6
urban 'decline', 100–1, 103
'urban divide', 4–5
urban environmental
  history, 76–7, 79–81, 88,
  90–1
urban governance, see
  governance
urban history:
  definition of, 1
  development of, 10–32
  nature and purpose of, 1–6,
    10–12, 21–2, 27–8, 32
Urban History Group, 21, 27,
  57
  see also scholarly networks
urban infrastructure, 81–2,
  84–8, 119–21, 124–7
urbanization, 1–8, 12–14,
  16–19, 28–32, 75, 107
urban networks, 2–5, 23–4,
  62–3, 66–7, 104, 115,
  119–28
urban planning, 13, 81, 90,
  103–4, 108, 119–28, 127
urban poor, 4, 13, 44–54,
  88–91, 98, 104–6
urban preservation, 17, 107–8
urban renewal, 101, 106, 122
urban renewal order, 18, 104,
  106, 125

urban turn, 12, 28–32
urban way of life, 14–15,
    16–17, 39, 92–4
Uruchurtu, Ernesto (Mexico
    City), 48

Venezuela, urban planning
    in, 122–3
Vertov, Dziga, 110–11
Vlugt, Willem de
    (Amsterdam), 62, 74
voluntary associations, 56, 62,
    65–7, 93, 127
Vries, Boudien de, 67

Wade, Richard, 17
walking, 108–13
Walkowitz, Judith, 101, 111
waqf, 66
Ward, David, 36–7
warehouses, 95
Warner, Jr, Sam Bass, 17, 20,
    35–6, 116
washerwomen, 54
waste-water, 71, 84–8
Water Aid, 52
water supplies, 29–30, 46,
    52–3, 59, 61, 66, 69, 73,
    80, 83–8, 125

waterworks, 83, 84–8,
    127
Weber, Adna Ferrin, 15
Weber, Max, 14–15, 66, 92
Weintritt, Otfried, 83
Western city, 15
wharfs, 80
Whiteley, William
    (London), 101
Wibaut, Floor
    (Amsterdam), 62
Wirth, Louis, 14, 16, 92
Wolff, Michael, 24–5
Woolworth's, 101
world history, 116–17
    see also global history;
        international history;
        transnational history
World's Columbian Exposition
    (1893) (Chicago), 26
World Trade Center (New
    York), 100
Worster, Donald, 77–8
Wright, Frank Lloyd, 103

Zhan, Shaohua, 7
Zhecun, Shi, 31
zoning, 19, 81, 107–8
    see also urban planning